T0199153

THE
CIRCUMCISED
Heart

Ready, Imperfect,
Softened, Transparent

MARILYN O. FLOWER

WESTBOW
P R E S S®
A DIVISION OF THOMAS NELSON
& ZONDERVAN

Scripture quotations are from The Holy Bible, English Standard Version®
(ESV®), copyright © 2001 by Crossway, a publishing ministry of
Good News Publishers. Used by permission. All rights reserved.

This book is a work of non-fiction. Unless otherwise noted, the author
and the publisher make no explicit guarantees as to the accuracy of
the information contained in this book and in some cases, names of
people and places have been altered to protect their privacy.

WestBow Press books may be ordered through booksellers or by contacting:

WestBow Press
A Division of Thomas Nelson & Zondervan
1663 Liberty Drive
Bloomington, IN 47403
www.westbowpress.com
1 (866) 928-1240

Because of the dynamic nature of the Internet, any web addresses or
links contained in this book may have changed since publication and
may no longer be valid. The views expressed in this work are solely those
of the author and do not necessarily reflect the views of the publisher,
and the publisher hereby disclaims any responsibility for them.

All photos are supplied by, and are the property of, the author.

ISBN: 978-1-5127-6082-8 (sc)
ISBN: 978-1-5127-6083-5 (hc)
ISBN: 978-1-5127-6081-1 (e)

Library of Congress Control Number: 2016917281

Print information available on the last page.

WestBow Press rev. date: 10/21/2016

Dedicated to my children and grandchildren
and to the memory of family and friends who
have passed into eternal life with Jesus.

CONTENTS

Introduction xiii

1. C: Character in Check 1
    A Visible Sign of God's Love 1
    God's Character 5
        Knowing and Understanding God 6
    Human Character 8
        God Checks Our Character 10
        Wanting to Change 14
    Character Checked 16

2. I: Identity Secure 18
    God Is Who He Says He Is 18
    Whose We Are 20
        Whom We Follow 21
        Whom We Worship and Adore 22
        Whom We Obey 23
    Spiritual Identity Crises 25
        Identity, Faith, and Travel 26
    God Provides 30
        Facing Challenges as God's Child 34
    Discerning Identity 35
    Identity Secured 37

3. R: Relationships Right 39
    Birth and Ancestry 39
    Family Matters 42

From Child to Adult..43

Relationship with God..45

God Loves Me!...47

    Names Matter...50

Personal Relationship with God............................53

    Learning to Be His Child..............................56

    Father and Child..58

    Obedience and Discipline..............................59

Relationships God's Way.......................................61

4. C: Childlike Trust..63

    In His Image...63

    Childhood Faith..65

        Costly Prosperity.....................................67

    The Narrow Gate...69

        Abraham Ulrikab's Story...........................70

        Curiosity, Creativity, and Critical Thinking...72

    Birth and Rebirth...74

        Part of the Family....................................76

    Trusting God as His Child..............................77

        Trusting with a Circumcised Heart..............78

    A Child's Trusting Heart...............................82

    God's Will, God's Word, God's Way................84

5. U: Unseen Priority..85

    Fear of the Unseen.......................................85

    An Emotional Sign.......................................87

    The Meaning of Life.....................................88

    The Spiritual Dimension...............................88

        Spiritual Experiences, 1984.........................90

        Healing, Spring 2004...............................91

        Theological Study, 2005–2008....................93

Coincidences or God Speaking? 94

The Unseen Is Priority 97

6. M: Matter Is Secondary 101

Liaison between Spirit and Matter 101

Teaching and Learning 104

Learning God's Will and Ways 105

Physical Existence Is a Gift from God........... 106

Unseen Intersecting Matter......................... 107

The Creator and His Creation.............................. 109

Matter as Priority.. 109

Priority Matters... 111

God First 112

7. C: Courage in Christ 114

Courage to Stand 115

In the World, Not of It 115

Courage of Commitment............................. 116

Courage to Uphold the Truth 117

Courage in a Dying World.................................... 118

God's Encouragement 121

Courage to Live for God 122

New Growth after the Fire 123

Take Courage Courageously 127

Courage to Proclaim.................................... 129

Clarity and Confidence 130

Courage for the Journey 131

8. I: Intentional Intimacy.. 132

What Is Love? 132

God's Love.. 134

Love Says I Am Sorry 135

God's Perfect Intimacy.. 135

    Loving as God Loves 137

    A Woman's Love.. 138

The World Does Not Love Us................................... 140

The Marriage Covenant... 141

Intimacy of Heart 142

Walking in God's Intentional Intimacy................... 145

    Intimacy God's Way.. 147

9.   S: Sanctification Proceeding................................... 149

Justification, Sanctification, and Glorification 149

Tension: The World Versus God's Love and Laws.. 151

    Readiness of Heart.. 152

    Imperfect and Desiring Change...................... 153

The Sword of God 154

A Circumcised Heart 156

Sanctification.. 162

    Wisdom of the Heart....................................... 163

10. E: Eternal Expectations.. 166

Promise and Expectation... 166

Expect to Question 167

Expect to Be Known by Your Fruits........................ 167

    All Are Called... 169

    Expect the Unexpected 170

Expectation: A New Heart....................................... 172

    Learning God's Way.. 173

    Witness and Service.. 175

    Not Expecting an Easy Life 177

No Fear... 178

Assurance.. 179

Expectation in the Last Days................................... 180

11. D: Dedication to God...................................... 183

    Wisdom Is God's Will............................. 184

    Discerning God's Will 186

        Loving and Obeying God........................ 188

        To Whom Much Is Given........................ 189

        Relinquishing My Will for His 190

    Surrendering Our Wills 192

    A Woman Serving God.......................... 193

    Dedicated to God's Ways....................... 196

12. ❧: The Circumcised Heart: Ready, Imperfect,
Softened, Transparent 199

    A Drastic Change of Heart 201

        Readiness Is Essential 203

        Imperfect—Sanctification Proceeding.......... 204

        Softening—The Holy Spirit at Work 205

        A Transparent Heart.................... 206

    God's Truth Sets Us Free 207

    God's Truth Brings Joy, Peace, Love, and Hope 209

    Each Child of God Has a Circumcised Heart 211

    The Circumcised Heart 213

INTRODUCTION

God is light and in him is no darkness at all. (1 John 1:5b)

God is the light of the world. He is the light of my life. There is no sin in him, but there is in me. Ten years ago I would not have envisioned how God would fashion everything in my life to converge as it has. God has taught me to trust him and his Word (the Bible) completely, through the power of the Holy Spirit. Living my life through the lens of the Bible I find much more light and greater joy than I ever did living for myself, and I am much better equipped to handle darkness when I am tempted.

This book blossomed out of a tangible sign from God in January 2008 which flowed from his perfect love. It is an account of how God's amazing love has spoken to me throughout my life. I grew closer to God through two marriages, the first to Corb, the father of my two grown children, who died in 1984, and the second to Stephen, an Anglican priest who encouraged me to do theological study, who died in 2011. God's love consoled, supported, and motivated me, amid loss, trial, pain, and darkness, but especially after beginning theological study in September 2005.

In January 2008 God got my full attention. I began to look on life with new eyes and, since then, I have done things I never thought I would do. Prayer, reflection, and many hours examining the Bible has helped me partially understand what the sign from God means. I believe that God gifted me with this sign, unworthy as I am, to encourage me to continue to work to know him better so that I would be better equipped to share his love with others.

My life ever since has been committed to serving him. I will never fully understand why this happened to me, but it has changed my life completely.

This is my story illuminated by what the biblical metanarrative has taught me about God and about me. I include some Bible passages, what they mean, and what they have done for me and in me, but God's story is only complete in the totality of the Old and New Testaments as one work. The Bible is a finely orchestrated symphony, every book holding equal weight, culminating in a majestic crescendo describing who God is, who we are as his children, and how he means for us to live life on earth.

This book was conceived during a two-week spiritual retreat that Stephen and I took to Mazatlán, Mexico, February 26 to March 13, 2010, following a church-planting conference in Dallas-Fort Worth, Texas. In the spring of 2007 I had completed a Master of Theological Studies degree and had written a thesis as part of the degree requirements. That exercise gave me a desire to do further theological research and writing because my comparison of an African and Western exegesis of Revelation 12 revealed a wealth of biblically sound theological writings done by third-world theologians. This process had been a phenomenal experience for both me and Stephen, who read and commented on most of my writing. We planned to write a book encouraging couples to study the Bible while they developed meaningful relationships with Jesus and with each other. We wanted others to be blessed by a strong marriage through faith in God and a growing knowledge of the Bible, as we were. I would do the writing and Stephen the illustrations.

Early in our marriage, in the late 1990s, we had talked about writing much-needed Christian children's books. We had developed animal characters and a brief storyline and done some preliminary sketching. Our thoughts turned to writing for adults when our own faith was tested by Stephen's cancer diagnosis in the fall of 2002. Our faith was further challenged by church issues in 2007 and 2008. The sign of January 2008 did not affect Stephen to the extent it did me, but it increased a desire in both of us to draw closer to God and be obedient to him. While we were in Mexico, we began the book for adults.

After arriving home, we were busy with work and church commitments and Stephen's suspicions that his prostate cancer was no longer under control were realized. The book was set aside. We returned to it a year later in early March 2011, when an alternative approach to treating Stephen's aggressive, terminal cancer was working so well that for three months the disease retreated formidably. The oncologist advised us to continue what we were doing. My thoughts and writing turned to God's mighty power to heal.

Since Stephen's initial diagnosis I had researched and implemented many natural homeopathic remedies for fighting cancer, but when traditional medicine seemed to be working, they were not followed. After returning from Mexico in March 2010 we initiated a regimen that included natural aloe vera, essiac tea, and immune-boosting supplements. An organic vegan diet, including vegetable juicing, based on an alternative medicine course on plant-based nutrition from the T. Colin Campbell Foundation I had taken online through Cornell University, after reading the bestseller *The China Study* (2006), was the foundation. We believed that God was healing Stephen physically and that our writing would describe the complex protocol which, with God's guidance and direction, had cured his body of advanced cancer.

A physical cure, however, was not God's will. The book was again set aside in October 2011 after Stephen's death. I questioned if writing was even part of God's plan for my life. I did not know what God wanted, but his call on my life was strong. If I had been born male, there would have been no conflict in my mind; I was not, and there was conflict. I was ordained to the diaconate in 2010 soon after returning from Mexico, and although I felt some spiritual fulfilment in being a coach for a program at a men's prison, I still questioned aspects of my call to ministry, mainly associated with my gender, and especially after Stephen's death.

November 2011 to the summer of 2014 was a whirlwind of activity as I oversaw the building of, and move into, a new house, dealt with my father's and stepson's hospitalization and my father's subsequent death, cared for two of my granddaughters periodically, continued with volunteer work at the prison, took trips to Israel in February 2012 and January 2014, trained to lead a two-year Bible study for my church, among much else. During 2012 God placed a Christian woman in my life who led me to a group of African women who met weekly for Bible study and prayer. They needed someone to oversee their group, and I agreed to do that. My own personal Bible research of Jesus's relationship with women, mainly involving New Testament characters, grew into our study. It proved to be as much for me as it was for the group, because it helped me resolve reservations about ordination to the priesthood.

I resumed writing in the fall of 2014 after ordination, but greater clarity came in the spring of 2015 when I was halfway through the Old Testament portion of an intense two-year Bible study program. Reflecting again on my spiritual journey, especially in light of my unfolding understanding of the Old relative to the New Testament, I found a renewed energy to write the things I felt God pressing me to write. I felt that God wanted me to write, not just for my use—I find journaling therapeutic and life-enriching for that—but his.

Throughout my study I contemplated and questioned my life and beliefs compared to those of mainstream Western Christianity and to God's Word. The process of reliving painful personal events was physically, mentally, spiritually, and emotionally onerous. It caused me to completely rely on God through Jesus in the power of the Holy Spirit while honestly reflecting on my past in the reality of the present and contemplating God's plan for my future. Although God is Spirit outside of time, he uses our physical bodies through life experiences in chronological time to teach us his truth. Through it all I realized that God's love for me, his patient endurance with me, and his reworking my mind, heart, and spirit to yield my will to his will and his plan for my life is the ultimate love story.

The original book Stephen and I planned to write was to have a missional focus at a time when much of the institutional church in the West had turned from holding God's Word as *the* reliable guide for life. Juxtaposed to this, the much less prosperous third-world church stood strongly and firmly in their Bible-based faith, despite their stand jeopardizing funding sources. The second book was to be based on Stephen's healing. When God did not heal Stephen, my focus became the much deeper spiritual healing found in dying and being present with Jesus. My plan was to include my healing after grief, about which I was becoming more knowledgeable directly and through my relationship with God and his Word.

This, the third book, has the missional focus of the first book, with the added experiential evidence of God's hand on my life. I always knew God's hand was on me, but now my eyes were opened. God directed me to take the emphasis off the person being healed, physically, emotionally, or spiritually, and place it on the Divine Healer and his Word, as it should be. What God requires of believers and how he instructs us and communicates with us necessitates our being true and loyal to him and his Word.

I refocused on the mystery of God's love for me through the 2008 sign which I, unsuccessfully, had tried to ignore. This sign was more than just an object—it had significantly enhanced my relationship with my transcendent God. Although I did not speak often of this sign, it was never far from my heart; it became a greater part of my thoughts especially after Stephen's death, as I pored over the Old Testament. This is the story that God, not me, wanted told. I wanted my writing to be theological, not personal.

Stephen and I did not have a title for our book. My first title addressed our prayer for healing: *God Wants You Well: Healed of Cancer*, then *God Wants You Well: The Ultimate Healing: A Personal Journey*. When I allowed God's will to override mine and my writing in mid-2015, I began *Circumcision of the Heart: Intersected by His Perfect Love*. In September 2015 as I finished the first draft and prepared to leave for Israel for Sukkot, I knew the title would be *The Circumcised Heart: Ready, Imperfect, Softened, Transparent*, as it described what a heart turned toward God, a circumcised heart, might look like. At first *transformed* was the last word in the title, but we are never totally transformed in this life. Total honesty and transparency in all matters, however, are essential to a circumcised heart.

Upon returning from Israel on October 9, I started rewriting the rough draft I had completed before leaving St. John's on September 21, but my work was far from polished as I struggled with how much God wished me to divulge. Keeping everything private would have been my selfish will, not his. I would have preferred to use a pseudonym, but there is no anonymity with God. In the end God directed what I should reveal.

This book is to and for God's honor and glory. It is a testimony to his unending love and faithfulness. My children and grandchildren will have a record of what God has done for, in, and with me, although they may not understand it. Any royalties are directed to Open Doors, an international organization distributing Bibles freely to persecuted Christians and offering Bible training worldwide. The Bible is the most precious possession anyone can have.

My strength comes from the power of the Holy Spirit and is reinforced through the supremacy and sufficiency of the Bible. God blessed me with a grandmother who further strengthened my love for Jesus, birth parents who taught me I could do or be anything, two wonderful husbands who loved me far more because they first knew and loved God, a son who learned well the importance of family responsibility through his father and grandfather, a daughter who gifted and privileged me to be present for the birth of her two daughters, and the biblically faithful believers I know and love who love God and the Bible as I do. For the past four and a half years, I have enjoyed in-depth Bible study with some as eager to study it as I am. I thank them for their joy, open-mindedness, and faithfulness in learning with me more of God and his Word.

I am especially blessed by three faithful women of prayer I meet with weekly, and for one very special biblically minded friend. Thank you very much Anne, Eleanor, Trudy, and Iona for your friendship, honesty, and devotion to God and the Bible. I am especially appreciative to Iona Bulgin, who unselfishly offered to edit this work. Thank you, Iona, for pushing me beyond my comfort zone and encouraging me to write the hard things with love, those things I felt God prodding me to write that I could only do in his strength. Words are insufficient to express the depth of my gratitude. God alone knows the tremendous amount of work this has been for you—a real work of heart.

I know firsthand the pain of journeying with a loved one living with a terminal illness. I know the toll on caregivers, even those who know, love, and follow Christ. I also know the pain that comes solely from day-to-day living—hurting and being hurt. In recent years I know the stigma associated with loving God, the Bible, and answering God's call to ministry. It is my responsibility to communicate any knowledge I gained from living for Christ and sharing the truth of the Bible that may strengthen and encourage others, especially regarding their Christian walk. I see the Holy Spirit working in his faithful flock.

I empathize with those staring death in the eye, either personally or through a loved one, but this book will not ensure anyone's spiritual well-being. I do know who can and where to learn about him. The Bible *must* be the guide. Everything and everyone else must be verified against it. Acceptance of Jesus as Lord, while looking honestly with a prayerful heart into God's Word under the guidance and direction of the Holy Spirit, is the answer. All adults, with the ability to, must be responsible for their own physical, emotional, and spiritual well-being, for which they will be held accountable.

This is not a work of fiction, although parts of it are otherworldly. It deals with issues and events which only a few years ago would not have been believed, as they did not fill the secular rational criteria of the day. Today the supernatural realm is more accepted, yet discernment is often lacking. Our bodies last briefly but our spirits are immortal, requiring proper and regular nourishment that is more important than good nutrition is for our bodies. Adequate biblical sustenance is essential to spiritual knowledge, wisdom, discernment, and sound judgment.

Even more difficult than health issues are those challenges followers of Christ face in a world that does not wish to hear of God's absolute truth. In the West generally everyone is shown tolerance and respect, except for those labeled in a pejorative, or derogatory, manner. Biblically faithful Christians are sometimes among this minority. Believers desire to be shown the same respect given to a follower of any other belief system, the opportunity to believe what they believe and to defend it—no different from those with faith placed solely in their human abilities, reason, and logic, really. While some self-proclaimed, well-educated, open-minded individuals have read the Bible, some have not, but they feel informed enough to criticize it. Thankfully God protects, guides, and encourages us, as he alone fully understands our trials. He empowers us as we stand for his hard truths against the world's easy wrongs, as we love our neighbors as he loves them, in all sincerity and truth, and despite all circumstances.

Ultimately this book is based on true and genuine love. If we love God, our families, and our neighbors as ourselves, we must have enough integrity to be totally honest with them. This means speaking and teaching the truth calmly and peacefully with and in love. It also means listening to them respectfully, and with patience, as God does with us, and requiring the same of them. God protects and guides us to do this, providing just what we need when we need it.

My prayer is that anyone reading this book will desire to read and study God's Word for themselves. We are blessed to live at a time and in a place where we still can do that. Our well-being, quality, and enjoyment of life here and now, and, ultimately, our eternity and that of those we love, is far too precious to place precariously in the hands of others.

> Let the words of my mouth and the mediations of our hearts be acceptable in your sight, O Lord, our rock and our redeemer. (Psalm 19:14)

Marilyn O. Flower, Thanksgiving 2016

CHAPTER 1

C: CHARACTER IN CHECK

"For my thoughts are not your thoughts, neither are your ways my ways," declares the Lord. "For as the heavens are higher than the earth, so are my ways higher than your ways and my thoughts than your thoughts." (Isaiah 55:8–9)

*A*ll of the Bible is God-breathed and useful for teaching, rebuking, correcting, and training in righteousness. Yet the above passage has meant more to me than any other passage about who God is. Over and over I read and digest it as I struggle to know more about God and his ways. This passage is a fitting beginning to a book that examines what God has done *with* me, *for* me, and *in* me through his Living Word.

A Visible Sign of God's Love

On December 18, 2007, the Anglican bishop for Eastern Newfoundland and Labrador sent a letter to all of the denomination's priests, mandating that they attend a meeting on January 21, 2008. At this meeting, the invited priests would restate their ordination vows, sign a document indicating their loyalty to the new bishop rather than to his predecessor (who had relinquished his license due to theological issues with the church body), and be issued new licenses. That letter not only drew media attention worldwide through radio, television, newspaper, and Internet coverage, but it also affected me greatly. As a graduate with a master's degree in theological studies, I had concerns about present happenings in the church, both locally and nationally, regarding biblical interpretation. A late bloomer in terms of biblical study, I was by then realizing the Bible's bountiful treasure. It also affected me directly, as Stephen, my husband, was a pastoral leader in that denomination. And for similar issues in the early 1990s, my children and I had moved from our church to another denomination, despite our original church's ties to my first husband, Corb, and his family. I was shocked that it was happening again—this time in the denomination into which I was born. I was raised to believe in and love God, through Jesus, and the Bible with all of my heart and soul. I thought Anglicanism upheld the supremacy of the Bible.

As January 21 approached, my heart grew heavier. On Friday, January 18, my thoughts and my prayers were focused on the upcoming meeting as I contemplated how a church so closely aligned historically to the Bible could suddenly lose its allegiance to, and trust in, it and its author, God. The situation was probably exacerbated by a power struggle and confusion over what constituted essential doctrine. Faith issues were and still are primary to me. These issues, while uniting Christ's church, divide institutional church bodies.

That day I decided to make raisin tea buns. As a child I had watched my mother and grandmothers make molasses, raisin, and blueberry tea buns. I enjoy baking and find it therapeutic. It allows me to think about life, and on that day, about the specific church situation. Stephen was at work, and I was alone, at times praying aloud. I soon felt as if I were a cog in an assembly line. I rolled out a third of the batter, floured it, and using a small wine glass of an appropriate circumference, I cut out the buns one by one and placed them on a greased baking sheet. One baking sheet was ready to go in the oven. The third—and last—batch was floured, and I began cutting the buns for the second baking sheet. My mind was fully preoccupied with the Monday afternoon meeting.

Several times Stephen and I had talked about the situation and the decision that he faced. We contemplated what it would mean if he did not sign the document. After lengthy discussions with several others in the same dilemma, he decided he would sign the required declaration that would permit him to administer the sacraments within the church. At first I did not think I would attend the service, as I thought it was solely for clergy and invited guests. But when I discovered that it was open to anyone, I decided I would go.

As I cut out the last batch of tea buns, I realized just how troubled and agitated I was about the situation. I thought, *Oh dear God, if I feel like this, how sad you must be. Your heart must be broken.* With a heart that felt like it was breaking, I worked quickly and efficiently to finish cutting the tea buns. The glass went up and down over the dough, cutting out each little circle. *Sschwah-sschwah-sschwah.* I felt disassociated from my actions.

Pop!

The sound startled me back to reality, as I again became present in what I was doing. When I realized that the glass was broken, I became upset. *Now I've done it. I've broken the glass. The buns are ruined! This is what happens when I let my mind wander. Now I'll have to throw it all out. What a waste!* As I cleaned up the mess, I consoled myself, realizing that the buns on the first baking sheet were edible, as it was approximately a meter and a half from where I cut out the last batch; those in the cutting area and on the second sheet had to be discarded.

Holding the broken glass in my right hand while opening the garbage bin with my left, preparing to throw it in, I was startled to find that the glass was intact except for a perfectly heart-shaped hole in its side. Its rim was a complete circle. Feeling its fragility, and its strength, I was shocked to find that when I washed off the batter and dried the glass, it remained intact.

I felt God's presence; it was as if he was saying to me, *Marilyn, my heart, too, is broken. It is broken in two.* Beyond my rational understanding, God was communicating something to me. *God didn't feel the same gut-wrenching pain that I was feeling, did he?* He certainly knew exactly how I felt—I knew that. But why would he communicate his emotional pain to me in this way?

As I threw the dough into the garbage bin being careful not to cut my hands, I saw two large pieces of glass that, on closer inspection, fit together perfectly to fill the heart shape in the glass. Carefully washing the flour mixture off the pieces, I could not help but think, *Yes, God's heart is broken in two.*

I could not throw away the broken glass and the two pieces that had burst from it, but I was unsure of their significance, if any. My inclination was to scold myself for using a wine glass as a bun cutter. I also wondered if this was a sign from God or some other spirit; according to Matthew 12:39 and 16:4, an evil and adulterous generation seeks for a sign, but no sign will be given except that of the prophet Jonah. I concluded that no other spirit would want me to believe that God's heart was broken, and I knew that he cared enough for me to convey this message to me. I was not looking for a sign, although I was fervently praying. After all, I was only making tea buns.

When Stephen came home, I showed him the glass. He was speechless, but then he said jokingly, "We'd better not show this to anyone, or the next thing there will be a Church of the Broken

Heart," which was great comic relief. We did not have much time to talk about it since we were invited out for dinner and our hosts lived about a thirty-minute drive away.

I was not looking for a sign from God nor did I will it into being. It just happened. I was more bothered about why this would happen to me than whether I felt that God was expecting me to act on it or not. My life was hectic enough. We were in the process of moving. I had already boxed many kitchen items, and that was why my selection of glasses for bun cutting was limited. I put the glass in the back of the cupboard and pushed all thought of it to the back of my mind.

GOD'S CHARACTER

God is perfectly independent of us, yet he is a shield for all who take refuge in him. I have taken refuge in him. He is part of my life, not merely looking on from a distance in heaven. I have learned that, in addition to being the only uncreated Being and perfect love, God is much more. While some theologians may compartmentalize God's attributes as either communicable (meaning that humans may have similar qualities) or incommunicable (only possible with God), I believe that *how* we categorize God's character is unimportant. What is essential is that we understand that God is an active and loving part of our lives—although his nature and attributes vastly differ from ours. Anything that we think we may have in common with him, we do not; he alone is God—we are his beloved creation.

As a young child I was fascinated by the big words that described God, but I had trouble understanding them and keeping them straight. God's attributes are as complex and limitless as he is. He is omnipresent, or everywhere present; omniscient, all-knowing;

and omnipotent, all-powerful. He alone is holy and sovereign. His ways are so much higher than my ways that I dare not even begin to compare myself with him or any of his qualities. God's aseity—his ability to be totally independent—means that he does not need you or me. He chose to create and love us, and he desires that we love, obey, and trust him. God created us so that we might have a relationship with him and love him for who he is—not because of what he can or will do for us. He owes us nothing; we owe him everything. He made us, and he is King of kings and Lord of lords of all creation. He does not live in manmade palaces, nor is he served by human hands as though he needed anything from us—since he himself gives life and breath to all creation.

God uses everything in his creation, including us, to further his will. All of nature worships and obeys him. God relates differently to different people at different times. He alone knows best, is immutable (unchangeable), impeccable (perfect), immanent (in the world), yet transcendent (outside time and space). It has been challenging for me to love and trust God fully, while embracing his mystery; but his gracious love won my heart. God is my rock, my fortress, and the center of my being. He lovingly pursues me to earnestly seek to know him better.

KNOWING AND UNDERSTANDING GOD

God will use whatever he chooses to draw people to him. The Bible, God's objective Word, gives us all that we need to know about God and encourage us to draw closer to him. Intermittently in the past I pursued God and sought to know him through reading the New Testament. Each time I walked away, I realized that I could not live my life without him. During those dark periods I learned more about him by reading more of the Bible than just the New Testament. The closer I got to God, the closer he came to me; the more I called out to him, the more I understood of his Word. As hard as I try and as well as I heed his Word, I will only know him partially in this life. Without God, we are incomplete. There is a space inside each of us that, if it is not filled with the Holy Spirit, leaves us susceptible to other loves. The Holy Spirit guides us to pray to be shielded from what the Bible says may distract us from loving God.

The Bible reveals God's character through creation first, then through his relationships with the Israelites, through Abraham, Moses, the kings, and the prophets, as recorded in the Old Testament. God is further revealed through Jesus and the Holy Spirit in the New Testament. John the Baptist, the apostles, the early church, and particularly Jesus help us understand more about who God is and how much he loves us.

The Bible shows that Jesus is God. Few dispute that Jesus walked the earth, but some attack his nature and his character. According to C. S. Lewis, Jesus can only be one of three things: dishonest, demented, or who he says he is. Through believing that Jesus is who he says he is, we know that he is far more than a great moral teacher. His love for humanity, resulting in his ultimate sacrifice—crucifixion on a cross—so that we might have eternal life, is far more than a good person's laying down his life for a friend. Christ's bodily resurrection broke the chains of evil, sin, and death. Jesus commands us to be more than merely good examples of humanity.

The world has many good models to follow, numerous philanthropies to do good works, and plenty of social clubs. These demand far less of us than faith in God does. They are also much better received by the world. The Bible, too, is what it says it is, all of it, not just selected parts; to deny part is to deny all and to deny Jesus as Lord. If Jesus believed all of the Old Testament and quoted and taught it, we must do no less. We come to know God through knowing and following Jesus and the Bible.

God is Creator and Master of the universe—man is not. Specialists in every imaginable discipline can never know everything there is to know about a topic. There is always someone ready to prove them wrong: "The one who states his case first seems right, until the other comes and examines him" (Proverbs 18:17). We are impudent if we claim to know God fully, or if we compare him to anything at all, regardless of our biblical literacy. Part of getting to know God and his character is realizing that he is in total control of everything, and many of his ways are mysterious and unknowable.

Human Character

In our finite human wisdom, we have gone to the depths of the sea and flown into outer space; we can send thoughts anywhere in the world, almost instantaneously, and yet we cannot save people when an oil rig is smashed to pieces in a storm; we cannot find a huge aircraft when it disappears; and we cannot cure the power and sting of death. Even the smartest, richest, youngest, most influential, and most religious people on the planet are totally unsuccessful in such endeavors. Our desire may genuinely be to help others, but we do not always have the ability or power to enforce it.

God's character is perfect; ours is not. God's ways and thoughts are holy; they are not ours, and never could be. God will eternally be the same. Conversely, our only hope of fullness of life now, and eternity with him, is to accept and love him. We can choose to accept him through Jesus, live according to his laws and standards, and be blessed, or reject him, live life our way, and be cursed:

Thus says the Lord: "Cursed is the man who trusts in
man and makes flesh his strength, whose heart turns
away from the Lord. He is like a shrub in the desert,
and shall not see any good come. He shall dwell in the
parched places of the wilderness, in an uninhabited
salt land. Blessed is the man who trusts in the Lord,
whose trust is the Lord. He is like a tree planted by
water, that sends out its roots by the stream, and does
not fear when heat comes, for its leaves remain green,
and is not anxious in the year of drought, for it does
not cease to bear fruit. The heart is deceitful above
all things, and desperately sick; who can understand
it? I, the Lord, search the heart and test the mind, to
give every man according to his ways, according to
the fruit of his deeds." (Jeremiah 17:5–10)

Accepting Jesus as Lord of our lives will result in our drawing
closer to him and desiring to learn about his character and what he
expects of us. It will result in not only our loving him enough to
admit it when we rebel against him, grieving him through sin and
disobedience, but our sin will hurt us too as we begin to understand
how it hurts God. Our awareness of sin will cause us to repent and
turn from what grieves him. By getting to know God through Jesus,
we begin to get to know ourselves and what God expects of us.
Gradually, through reading the Bible, I learned what God expected
and knew how far I fell short. I wanted to change. The Holy Spirit
helped me grow into the person God desired me to be. I do not
remember the exact moment, as a child, I gave my life to Christ, but
I now know how my heart *was*, and still *is*, deceitful above all. God
searches, tests, and knows all hearts. He will help us resist sin and
keep us from self-delusion when we rely on him.

God made us to be dependent upon him. All desperately need God. If Jesus, fully divine and fully human, needed God and regularly prayed to him, crying out in his trials and temptations, how much more do we need to communicate with and cry out to him in the storms of our lives. We must cry out for strength to live as he commands so that we can resist worldly lures, avoid satisfying ungodly appetites, and be granted forgiveness when we confess our sin.

God made us to be intelligent, rational beings with the desire to relate with him. We must read his Word and understand his laws in order to know him and his standards. God also gave us free will, the ability to choose or reject him, to love him or not, but he will not force us to love him. God gave us dominion over creation; we are to care for all of his creation—his way. Loving God, being good stewards, and showing love to others is easier when we believe that God is a God of goodness, righteousness, justice, graciousness, and mercy; when he is perceived as angry and jealous, many reject him. They do not want to follow God if he is against worldly beliefs and standards, which he is.

God's anger, jealousy, and wrath are as much a part of his character as his love, kindness, and mercy. They are all perfect in every way, as he is perfect. God is perfectly just. He does not rely on our human logic or reasoning. God made the universe in all its complexity. Nothing escapes his watchful eye. Like I once did, many want to make their own rules. For years I did not abide by God's laws, nor did I want anyone to tell me what to do.

GOD CHECKS OUR CHARACTER

The Holy Spirit convicted me as I read and studied parts of the New Testament years ago, but recently I have been checked through reading the Old Testament prophets. Jeremiah, one of my favorites, tells us that if we depend on men and refuse to trust God, we will be cursed and have tormented lives. But if we turn to God and trust him, we will be blessed, spiritually and eternally, although our lives still may be difficult.

The choice to trust God is deeply personal. I have had faith in God for as long as I remember, but I found it far more difficult to give my life completely to him. Totally trusting him and giving him full rein in my life came gradually over the past decade after I realized that I could not live without his help. When I felt weakest, God showed me his mighty power and strength. At such times I felt that he was exposing those things in me that were displeasing to him and that separated me from him. I needed to repent of those sins. Such calls to repentance have drawn me closer to him, sealing my dependence on him and confirming my commitment to serve him.

God tested the patriarch Abraham, who trusted him enough to offer up his son Isaac, through whom God said Abraham would be the father of a great nation. Isaac was not sacrificed on the pyre; God figuratively raised him from the dead, a foreshadowing of his own son's sacrifice for us. God knew Abraham's heart. For most of my life I have had difficulty with this story. I could not understand how a loving God would expect such extreme devotion to him. I had difficulty identifying with a parent who would sacrifice his own son. In terms of plausibility of the narrative I could not understand how an animal could appear out of nowhere. That is—not until my second trip to Israel in January 2014, around Beersheba, when I visited the Negev Desert and saw how the horns of small animals could easily get stuck in the thicket of a large broom shrub or small tree. It was a watershed moment as I rethought my faith in light of the Old Testament narrative. If I had disobeyed God's promptings to study the Old Testament and go to Israel three times, I would have missed out on the tremendous blessings he had in store for me.

Marilyn O. Flower

En Avedat National Park in the Negev, January 16, 2014

Since the glass incident I have had many moments of clarity about my erroneous thinking about God's Word while reading the Old and New Testaments, while communicating with him in prayer, through Bible study and discussion with other Christians, and in Israel. I realized I had been putting my will ahead of his. I now know that God is to be fully trusted.

God knows the propensities for good and for evil within each of us, but he will not force his will upon us. Rejecting God may ensure a more contented and prosperous worldly life, but what will happen when this life is over? Once we reject God we have no further option—we do not know when we will draw our last breath or Jesus will return, and then we will have no opportunity to accept him. If we choose rejection, we are rejected, much like the tormented rich man was rejected (Luke 16:19–31).

Some people may desire God solely to obtain eternal life while still living for themselves. I believed that I could live my way, but biblical passages repeatedly showed me how that was impossible. Throughout the Old Testament, God warned Israel not to adopt the sinful customs of the surrounding nations, stressing that they were to have no involvement with idol worship or the occult. Marrying a Gentile was forbidden. Infractions against God's laws and commandments were severe (e.g., David and Bathsheba [2 Samuel 11:1–12:13], King Ahab and Jezebel [1 Kings 21], and Aaron's sons [Leviticus 10:1–3]). Despite this God often used Gentiles to accomplish his will: Ruth, ancestor of Jesus (Ruth 1–4), and Rahab, the prostitute (Joshua 2–6). Repeatedly Israel disobeyed God. Like them we too are stiff-necked and rebellious. We too harden our hearts toward God as we proceed to live in our own strength to get our own way.

God loved us so much that he sent his Son, Jesus Christ, to die for us. He commands our love and obedience, as he did in

Old Testament days. Jesus offers salvation to all who come, and in combination with the Holy Spirit and the Bible, God provides all the spiritual nourishment, strength, perseverance, and fortitude we require to change from our sinful ways. What is pleasurable to our flesh is often sinful to God. Such pleasures pale in comparison to the joy of knowing God. Focusing on Jesus, who endured the cross for us, we have everything necessary to travel the straight and narrow path to God. The Bible clearly delineates what is expected. With the Holy Spirit's indwelling, believers listen to his prompting to turn away from temptation and sin. They earnestly repent and seek forgiveness.

WANTING TO CHANGE

The Bible teaches us who we are as sinners and helps us understand those areas that please and displease God. It describes the solution for our sinful human condition: Jesus. We are blessed to be able to read the Bible for ourselves. Each one of us can have his or her own copy and/or audio copy of it—not just the laws, prophets, and writings of the Old Testament that Jesus studied in his day but the entire Bible, both New and Old Testaments, God's Word, which must not be added to or taken away from. Believers have the complete written Word of God in addition to his indwelling Holy Spirit. Although we have the works of the church fathers, who dedicated their lives to help us turn our hearts to God and know and love him through his Word, the Bible is our sole source of absolute truth. We are blessed to be living at a time when information is readily accessible, but we have the formidable responsibility to discern what is of God so that we may walk with him and be a witness of his love to others.

Making changes in my own strength worked, but only to a certain extent—they did not satisfy my deepest longing to be close to God and to be loved as I never could be by another person. I am thankful that God is exceedingly patient and loved me sufficiently, despite my sinfulness, to get my attention, draw me closer to him during difficult times, and cause me to want to change according to his will. I had to trust God, his Word, and the Holy Spirit—not me.

We often do not have choices about what happens in our lives, but we do have a choice of attitude. We always have a choice to search God's Word and bring everything to him in prayer. We can choose to be kind, generous, and love people and to witness and minister to others' physical, emotional, and spiritual needs, as Jesus did. These help build a Christ-like heart that God desires within each of us.

When people hit rock bottom, they may not change, because they see no need for change. Sometimes they even believe their own lies. A change of heart bringing new life is only possible when we accept Jesus, welcome the Holy Spirit, and allow him to convict us, through God's Word, of our sin. Wanting to change is often a more difficult step than the change itself, because the lure of the world is powerful, and living in the flesh takes little effort. Sound biblical doctrine, in conjunction with God's love in action through others' ministering to those in need, is required to bring lasting change.

I assist with some program facilitation and church services at our local men's prison. It is evident there how difficult it is to make changes without God's help, even when life is at its lowest. Throughout the years, greater numbers of men have told me how being in prison has made them rethink what is most important, as they begin to reconsider God. Some have said prison saved their lives, physically and spiritually. While some had never opened a Bible before being incarcerated, some could quote biblical passages but their understanding of them sometimes was warped by misinterpretation. The men's honesty and forthrightness, in conjunction with sound

Bible teaching, has allowed the Holy Spirit to begin to transform those who sincerely want to change, even though they may have setbacks, and even reoffend. Real change requires sincere hearts, patience, and time.

When we allow God to change our hearts, he changes us from the inside out; our character changes are evident to others. Not all people see the light of God's truth, which illuminates the darkness in a broken world, as positive. Believers live God's truth and love in tandem. When we turn our faces from God, and sin, we are convicted to repent and return to him again. All believers are vulnerable to temptation, but new believers are especially so. The love and support of godly mentors, in addition to regular Bible reading and prayer, are crucial to help new believers guard their character and withstand worldly temptations and enemy attacks.

CHARACTER CHECKED

God knows us, tests us, and demands a character change. He knows what we need and he uses everything to his glory to assist us. When we accept Jesus, we realize that we must change, but it requires effort. We ask for God's help and he enables us to change. The more we delve into God's Word, the closer we are drawn to him, but we also see how much more we need to study it. Accepting the Holy Spirit's character check is painful, but it is what God requires.

Jesus's character, like God's, is perfect. He shows no impartiality, for he died for all of humanity. He is the perfect teacher, who has given us difficult teachings. He told us to love our enemies and to pray for those who persecute us so that we may be sons of our Father in heaven. If we only love those who love us, we are no different from nonbelievers. Not only are we to love our enemies but we are also to seek righteousness. We are to teach the full truth of the Bible—anything less is unacceptable. Jesus set high standards, which he enforces, but he helps all who call on him sincerely.

I have learned that God is perfectly trustworthy. To my shame, I have not been totally obedient and submissive to his will, although I am learning to let him be God of all of my life. This is especially difficult, as I like to be in control. I know God will help me work on this for however long I am alive. God will help me when I call on him, but he will provide what he knows I need, not what I want or feel I need.

We must cry out every day for God to keep us from sinning. It is a constant struggle, with steps backwards and often much pain, but God is always near. We must aim for perfection, as our heavenly Father is perfect, while knowing that we can never achieve holiness. We have to be ever vigilant of who we are as Christians and of who it is that God desires us to be. Effort is required to deliberately calibrate ourselves against God's standard. Although we may forget about him, God is faithful: we are never out of his mind. When we love God, through Jesus, with our whole being, we welcome the Holy Spirit's guidance in resisting temptation, obeying, serving, and loving God, and working toward righteousness. God provides all that we need to keep our characters in check and help us draw closer to him, because he loves us.

CHAPTER 2

I: IDENTITY SECURE

See what kind of love the Father has given to us,
that we should be called children of God; and so we
are. The reason why the world does not know us is
that it did not know him. (1 John 3:1)

*G*od was, is, and forever will be perfect in every way. His love
sustains me, and I know that I am secure as his child. His love
will sustain all who call on him, enabling them to know who they
are too. Some parts of the church can be so busy propagating self-
serving, spiritual propaganda that they are unable to discern who
God is and how he reveals himself to the world. They, like others
who chase after false gods, do not know God himself. They do not
understand that believers are God's children, because they do not
know what that means.

GOD IS WHO HE SAYS HE IS

God is who he says he is, although he is incorrectly identified by
those who do not know him, his Word, or his Son. Every day
through reading the Bible I understand more clearly who God is as
Father, Son, and Holy Spirit, mainly through understanding who

Jesus is in his humanity. I find it easier to identify and relate with Jesus, who once lived an earthly life, than with God, who is Spirit, even though I have his Spirit dwelling inside me. This, I believe, is one reason that God, in his perfect wisdom, gave us Jesus as mediator and arbitrator. With every moment I am more astounded by God, as the Holy Spirit assures me of who I am in Christ as a child of God. God usually does not contravene the laws of the universe he set into motion, but he will do as he sees fit—ultimately sending his Son to earth in full humanity.

God tells us in Malachi 3:6 that he does not change, but he is so great that we will never fully know him. God's Word also will never change. We need to be careful when we are talking about God, because his truth is often distorted. How we define God does not affect who he is, but it does reveal our biases. Our descriptions of God must be biblical; otherwise they are either reactionary or self-serving. Bible believers are often perceived as hateful and judgmental, especially about such issues as abortion, birth control, sexuality, and dying. Rather than the church's correcting misconceptions with biblical truth, some swing the doctrinal pendulum to the opposite end. By doing this, a false Christ or gospel is taught. Jesus stands firmly on God's Word. In our zeal to be loving, we must not cast God's Word aside.

Our understanding of God is a reflection of who we believe he is based on who we believe we are. Who we believe God is impacts how we relate to him and may eventually influence others. If we do not know God as he reveals himself in the Bible, although we are created in his image, we may not be his children. Far more important than the question "Who am I?" in terms of spiritual identity to those of us who profess Christ is, "Whose am I?" and "Whom do I follow?" When we know whose we are and whom we follow, we know whom we worship, adore, and obey.

WHOSE WE ARE

Most people desire self-gratification. More and bigger lotteries offer instant, easy, glamorous lifestyles. Many seek a big win despite winners' lives being ruined and fortunes evaporated. Words, definitions, and concepts of identity are constantly in flux, mirroring culture's instability, but God and his Word never change.

Our primary identity derives from our families. Because of genetic engineering, reproductive technologies involving surrogacy, frozen sperm and egg banks that are largely unregulated, and artificial insemination, increasingly more people are growing up not knowing the identity of one, or both, biological parents. This unsettles many, as evidenced by those seeking long-lost family members and researching their ancestry.

In the twenty-first century identity can be fluid. A person, however, is more than the sum of his or her genes. It includes character, cultural beliefs, books read, places visited, Internet sites followed—everything about us. Our identity especially impacts our relationship with God; for believers, it is impossible to define ourselves outside of God. Because we are body *and* soul, believers need to pay adequate attention to the Holy Spirit, which God breathes into the soul of every believer. When we ignore, stifle, or deny the Holy Spirit, we disobey God. Everyone saved by Christ has the Holy Spirit inside them and know whose they are.

In my early teens I ran away from home for three to four hours because my father had said that he owned me. I believed that only God owned me. As immature as my faith was at that time, God was key to my identity. When we realize that our identity is only secure in relationship to him, we see how simple it is to be rightly identified with him as his child, because he holds us totally in his hands. God knows who Christ has saved and will save. He knows whose hearts are circumcised. Even when we do not know our biological parents, we can learn who God is and relate to him as Father. My views of life, the world, and God were impacted by my relationship with him, mainly through prayer and reading the Bible. God created us all with the potential to know him, but we are only his children after we accept his offer of adoption, when we agree to be his child, loving what he loves and hating what he hates.

My identity is based on being God's child. I am God's daughter, not by physical birth, ethnicity, or anything I have done, but by accepting Jesus as my Lord and Savior. The Holy Spirit guides me to become a new creation. Regardless of today's preoccupation with and confusion about identity, Christ is the believer's identity, the Savior of the world. I rejoice in knowing that I am God's daughter.

WHOM WE FOLLOW

Acknowledging our addictions, harmful habits, grief, and other losses is important because we change only after we accept them as part of us. Our intellect enables us to reason and think morally, but it is our souls that connect our minds and hearts to God and enable us to think and act more like he does. Acknowledging every aspect of who we are, especially sinful things, known only to us and God, is necessary to all who desire to repent of their sin, and change.

When Christians step outside God's will and laws, they experience guilt as a result of conflict between what they believe and what they do. Walking apart from him becomes easier with each repeated sin. The conscience becomes dulled, seared perhaps, and no longer sounds the alarms that it would if nourished with prayer and God's Word. Trying to live more and more in the world while professing to follow Christ results in inner conflict, the chasm becomes too wide to straddle, and a decision must be made as to which master to serve. Will Jesus be Lord and Master or will sin, the flesh, the world, with the devil in control, master us?

Christians know whom they follow and their faith grows stronger due to the indwelling of the Holy Spirit. They model his example for living and teach his teachings. Some people, however, profess to know and follow Jesus. They expect the eternal reward of heaven yet do not accept the biblical Jesus and what he teaches about how Christians are to live. But we are only secure as children of God if we have acknowledged Him as Father and Jesus as Lord and Savior and follow his ways. No Christian hides his or her identity in Christ. Christians know whom they follow, rejoice in following him, and joyfully witness their faith to the world. Knowing whose we are and whom we follow results in a natural outpouring of love and adoration to God and honest love to family, neighbors, friends, and even our enemies.

WHOM WE WORSHIP AND ADORE

I worship God for I know I am his. I am secure in him who formed my inward parts and knit me together in my mother's womb. I praise God that I am fearfully and wonderfully made. I worship God as Jesus Christ teaches. His atonement for my sins ensures me of new life now and eternal life in the kingdom to come. My worship involves prayer, Bible study, witnessing to others, and singing psalms, hymns, and choruses. Most biblical passages that I recall from childhood were sung as hymns. Psalm 23 has always comforted me. I do not know why these words had such impact or why they still elicit feelings of remarkable peace—sheep are such dirty, smelly creatures. My heavenly Father's love and guidance is ever-present:

The Lord is my shepherd; I shall not want. He
makes me lie down in green pastures. He leads me
beside still waters. He restores my soul. He leads me
in paths of righteousness for his name's sake. Even
though I walk through the valley of the shadow of
death, I will fear no evil, for you are with me, your
rod and your staff they comfort me. (Psalm 23:1–4)

God comforted and consoled me as I poured out to him what I
could not share with my parents or anyone. Having to leave my
first job because of sexual harassment caused me to draw closer to
God because more than human strength was required to take away
my pain and uncertainty. I felt God's strength and warm embrace
at such times.

When we understand that God knows and loves us, we want to
worship and adore him with our whole hearts. We want to know him
as much as we humanly can. As we worship and adore him, he draws
us closer to himself. God calls us to rejoice equally in corporate
worship and peaceful, private moments in his loving presence.

WHOM WE OBEY

Living for self, we obey no one. Our human nature is to be selfish.
Aphorisms like "know thyself" and "to thine own self be true"
resonated within me for years. We live in an all-about-me world.
The Bible admonishes us, especially in Romans 12:3–8, not to think
too highly of ourselves, but to be humble, and to search our hearts
so that we know ourselves in order to know God. As I understood
who I am in Christ as a child of God, I realized that I must put him,
not myself, first.

Christians, under the Lordship of Jesus Christ and the direction of the Holy Spirit, have free will to follow Jesus's model of prayer, self-discipline, and obedience. To obey God should be his children's greatest desire. As the Holy Spirit guides Christians, we should welcome his direction and be vigilant because the enemy attacks our weakest areas. We must regularly pray for God's direction and guidance, read and meditate on the Bible, and evaluate ourselves in light of it.

Following God as Jesus did does not mean following Jewish customs. Jesus died for all—Jew and Gentile, black and white, male and female. He knows whose hearts have been circumcised and are his. God's covenant of circumcision with Israel was a circumcision of the heart, as Deuteronomy 10:16 and 30:6 and Jeremiah 4:4 state. Jesus is the New Covenant fulfilment of the law and of the covenant of circumcision. He is the sacrifice for those believing in him for salvation. Acts 7:51 and Romans 2:29 and 4:11–12 are especially pertinent. Jesus did not come to abolish God's laws or ways but to fulfil them. His and God's ways are one, just as Jesus and the Father are one.

Despite my knowing that I was a child of God, I did not deny myself wholly because I did not know that it was important; denial, sin, and repentance were rarely taught in church and became increasingly unpopular generally. Much teaching in the church today rests on the belief about God whereby a person can live life one's own way, as I did, and still go to heaven. Although I often felt uncomfortable about this, through my relationship with God and reading the Bible my conscience was pricked. I no longer desired to live for myself as I once did. God, through the Holy Spirit, gradually gave me the strength to obey him more and more. Through pouring out my heart to God and searching his Word, I realized that self-denial is the beginning of saying "Yes" to Christ's gift of salvation and turning wholeheartedly to him.

Self-examination is essential to recognizing sinfulness so that we can earnestly repent and be reconciled to God. My father taught me, as an adolescent, the importance of preparing, by way of resolving any residual sins, before communion. Later, through the conviction of the Holy Spirit, I understood the full import of preparing myself, because I then desired fellowship with God before fellowship with all others. I realized that what I delighted in and who I lived for must change if God truly was my Father. I delighted more in him and his will, meditated on his ways day and night, and delighted less in the ways of the world. Every day found me closer to God and his Word, as the Holy Spirit guided me to be obedient.

As we struggle with all that life brings, we change. Changing to be more like Christ is vital to a relationship with him. Sometimes God extraordinarily changes something, as with miraculous healings, but such interventions are not the norm nor are they always recognized when they do occur. Trials and crises of adversity, although they inflict pain, often result in exponential spiritual growth.

SPIRITUAL IDENTITY CRISES

Extreme circumstances sometimes result in unbelievers coming to know God quickly and intimately as Paul did in his remarkable conversion experience. Others, however, are angry and tell God to leave them alone. Some, oblivious to the God who loves them, continue to refuse to believe that he exists. Each crisis either leaves us stronger as Christians or we walk away from God for a time, even forever. My spiritual crises have always been worth the pain, but they pale compared to those of others. I have talked with Christians converted from other faiths who found the truth of God's Word too compelling to ignore and were forced to leave their homelands. Some came to Christ through visions, and subsequently studied and loved the Bible, but cannot return to their country. Their faith costs them far more than it ever cost me. Secure now as children of God, they are united as brothers and sisters with all believers throughout the world, especially with those who suffer for their Christian beliefs.

March, a month of birthdays in my family, is a time of celebration, fresh hope, and new ideas. The month contains several birthdays sandwiched between mine at the beginning and, for over a decade, Stephen's near the end of the month. Birthdays and other celebrations cause a person to reflect on life's meaning and purpose. March is a time to look forward to summer, the garden, and new life. It is also close to the celebration of Christ's resurrection and Pentecost. Jesus did, as the Jewish world still does, celebrate Passover in the spring, his last Passover, the time of his arrest. I always loved travelling in the spring but during March 2011 Stephen and I were preoccupied with an alternative treatment plan for his cancer. Although travel was impossible for us, we contemplated our faith and reflected on previous travel experiences.

IDENTITY, FAITH, AND TRAVEL

In March 2010 Stephen and I had spent two glorious weeks in a spiritual retreat in Mazatlán, Mexico, preparing for my ordination on Pentecost, May 23, 2010. Our time of prayer, reflection, submission, and repentance was further blessed by the proximity of a chapel and Sunday worship there. During our retreat we concentrated on our identity in Christ and God's call on our lives. We left Mexico with a deeper commitment and devotion to God, although apprehensions over Stephen's health loomed darkly overhead. God knew we would need his strength in order to withstand all we would soon face. He knew the number of days Stephen had left.

Deep in thought and reflecting on our own earthly circumstances, especially Stephen's deteriorating health, and coinciding with Japan's devastating earthquake, aftershocks, tsunamis, and horrific nuclear problems resulting from the March 11, 2011, series of disasters, I finally listened to the prompting of the Spirit to pour out my heart and be obedient to God's call to write. The tragedies in Japan affected me more than the unrest and violence in the Middle East because I had spent six wonderful weeks in the summer of 1995 in Fukushima City and prefecture as one of twenty Canadian guests of the governments of British Columbia and Japan commemorating the fiftieth anniversary of Hiroshima and Nagasaki.

My time with the generous Japanese people is indelibly etched in my memory. Extremely polite and thoughtful, their strong cultural identity is tied to their Buddhist and Shinto beliefs. Their elaborate festivals and ceremonies are tied to a sense of obligation, honor, and shame and rests on their spiritual heritage. Never have I been shown more respect and dignity than I was by the Japanese people. Sleeping on tatami floors in their living rooms, where the butsadan or shrines were housed, piqued my curiosity about their religion and culture. A visiting female would not normally receive high honor in Japan. But because I was a school principal, I received the honor that the position warranted. Although I was far from home, family, and church, I felt God's protective hand on me. Since Corb's death, my prayer life had become much deeper and stronger and I relied on God for protection and guidance for me and my family. Alone in Japan, God was especially close.

The Japanese women were very friendly to me. Although the majority of them had learned English as a second language, communication between us was not always easy. I was intrigued, however, by their comments about their faith and their curiosity about Christianity. Several women noted they had heard that it cost nothing financially to be Christian, whereas their families spent enormous sums of money changing each letter of a relative's name into a new name so that their loved ones would be ensured of going to nirvana at death. I told them that Jesus is a gift but that opinions about faith, church traditions, and doctrine vary. Their responses to my questions about the worship of the multitude of Buddha statues throughout their prefecture and their respect for charms and their power indicated that perhaps they themselves did not know. Their respect of and belief in the prayer and strict meditation of the temple monks was stronger than their understanding of their statues of Buddha, but they could not express the tenets of their religion well, possibly due to language limitations.

The 2011 Fukushima crisis sent me to my knees for the Japanese who had befriended me in 1995. My heart went out to them in their suffering as I recalled our conversations of struggling to achieve a higher state of being through adversity, of which they now had plenty. Japan had been struck by many natural disasters since my visit there in 1995. As I reflected on their present and past circumstances, I thought of how God uses pain and suffering to draw us closer to him, but that he is personal and knowable through Jesus—a stark contrast to the Buddha statues and shrines.

In my travels I noticed that people of different ethnicities were extremely devout, maybe because I met them in churches or in places where their faith was on public display. Eye contact, body language, and gestures made spoken language unnecessary. One Mexican family I met on a tour of their modest home in exchange for our two-day-old box lunches still lingers in my mind. On an archaeological cruise to Honduras, Guatemala, and Mexico in the spring of 1988, our tour bus stopped to visit local families as we crossed the Yucatan Peninsula to visit the Mayan ruins on the other side. Those who desired it were invited inside a baked-mud hut to visit with the family. My short visit with this Mexican family was a life-changing event for me. The father was a cobbler with his shoe hospital on a small wooden bench in the back garden; his children and poultry ran around the small enclosed space which doubled as a vegetable garden. The mother was proud of her small simple home, which had no electricity or running water. Cooking was done in the garden, but an old electric stove, which stored kitchen items, and a picture of Jesus over an old table and chairs were treasured. The family's demeanor spoke loudly of their love for one another and their home that shone brightly through what we in the West label poverty.

As I recalled these various experiences, I reflected on God's plan for Stephen and me and the remainder of our lives. As I contemplated Japan and its current situation, as compared to Mexico, Spain in 1985, Europe, the Mediterranean, and the Caribbean (many of which I felt had strong Christian backgrounds), I thought of the importance of faith in God compared to Western standards of living. Thoughts of strength of character in the face of pain and adversity and also of life after death made me consider my own situation in light of my faith. God's hand of comfort, security, and support was on Stephen and me as he nurtured us through his Word and prayer for the last one and a half years of Stephen's life.

Travelling had to be curtailed during the early writing of this book as Stephen's disease worsened. Life revolved around basic needs but it did not stop us from dreaming and talking about travel. One word that Stephen and I coined during that spring was *kibet*, a play on "keep it," because sometimes we, especially those studying theology, can make things far too complicated, resulting in veering away from God's truth. It is important to keep things simple, but it is also imperative to be totally honest. Everyone needs to be given truth in simple terms. God's Word is truth, as God can only be honest.

My aim in life is to *kibet*: *kib*—keep it brief, *e*—easy to understand, and *t*—to the point.

GOD PROVIDES

One of my favorite names for God that he uses for himself is Jehovah Jirah, the God who provides. God has always provided so abundantly for me, sometimes what I had absolutely no idea I needed. One of my desires since theological studies was to visit Israel, but Stephen had no desire to go. I took my first trip to Israel from February 6 to 19, 2012, a few months after his death. That trip was the most meaningful and informative trip of my life and occurred at a critical time in my spiritual journey.

When I returned home almost two weeks later in the early morning darkness to about three feet of snow in my driveway and slid my luggage across the frozen expanse to the front door, I realized that I wanted to return to Israel soon, and not because of the snow. As it was so soon after Stephen's death, and I had been his caregiver for nine years, and intensely for almost a year and a half, I felt almost numb on my first Holy Land experience, but Israel was home, Jesus's home. I soon sought another tour with the same tour company.

One option included going with the group I had gone with before; the second, joining a group from the United Kingdom. The group I had travelled with on my first visit to Israel was doing an Old Testament Exegetical tour—but I wanted nothing to do with it. I was totally disinterested in the Old Testament: it made little sense to me. The New Testament was *the* Christian book, I thought, and what I knew. I made arrangements to go on the January 26– February 10, 2014, tour with the UK group. In December 2013, weeks before I was to leave, I was notified that my tour had been cancelled due to insufficient numbers. I was, however, rebooked on the Old Testament tour that was leaving about two weeks earlier than I was originally supposed to have left. I was so disappointed that I contemplated staying home, but my heart was set on seeing Israel again. The irony was that I would be back home around the time that I was supposed to leave and I would be going on a tour that I did not want to go on.

Well at Tel Beersheva National Park, January 15, 2014

The Old Testament tour, although shorter, was more life-changing than my first trip to Israel in 2012. My eyes were opened by the vast wealth of archaeological evidence supporting God's Word that I was surprised and embarrassed by my ignorance and close-mindedness. Visiting the Tomb of the Patriarchs in the Cave of Machpelah in Hebron, the traditional resting place for Abraham, Isaac, Jacob, Sarah, Rebecca, and Leah, the vast Desert of Zin in the Negev, and the possible location of the well outside the gate at Tel Beersheva, where Abraham made a treaty with Abimelech, as recorded in Genesis 21:22, just before the account of Isaac's near sacrifice, leaves me speechless. I did not know such sites supporting the biblical accounts of God's covenantal relationship with Israel existed. Ever since that trip I have committed to studying God's entire Word, including the Old Testament.

I did not want to go on that Old Testament trip, but God knew I needed to go. God gets his way and has a unique sense of humor while achieving it. I was beginning to understand what it meant to be his child.

> And Abraham lifted up his eyes and looked, and behold, behind him was a ram, caught in a thicket by his horns. And Abraham went and took the ram and offered it up as a burnt offering instead of his son. So Abraham called the name of that place, "The Lord will provide," as it is said to this day, "On the mount of the Lord it shall be provided." (Genesis 22:13–14)

Just as God faithfully provided Abraham with the lamb on Mount Moriah in place of Isaac, he provided the experience I needed to increase my faith and draw me closer to him for his good purposes. God the Father always knows best and provides what we need most—knowing whose we are. He knew Abraham and what he needed, and he knows me and what I need. I am delighted to call him Father and I am blessed to be his child. As his children, we all have the same relational value in his eyes, regardless of age, gender, or skin color. We need only accept Jesus's offer to be God's chosen, adopted children.

FACING CHALLENGES AS GOD'S CHILD

Although I will never know in this life, I believe Corb's identity in Christ was secure, but we did not have the in-depth, theological discussions that Stephen and I had had. Corb was thirty-three when he died. I was thirty-one and my faith immature. Neither of us regularly or intensely read the Bible. We did not often have the deep, spiritual discussions of a mature Christian couple, although we regularly attended, were actively involved in, and supported a church.

If Jesus had not carried me after Corb's death in 1984, I believe I would have taken my own life. But the Holy Spirit dwelled in me and, gradually, I became a much more faithful child of God. Knowing I was living with the Holy Spirit in me not only gave me purpose but it also made Stephen's cancer diagnosis in 2002 and subsequent battle more bearable, as I was not carrying the load by myself. Stephen and I were both well equipped to live with his cancer because of our previous cancer experiences, but mostly due to our deep faith in Jesus. At the beginning of our cancer journey we felt that people diagnosed with cancer had few choices, but we soon questioned that assumption.

It is impossible to relate my journey without reflecting on those values and life experiences that Stephen and I shared, especially in 2010/2011. My work reflects Stephen's impact on my life. As we were primarily people of strong faith, with Jesus as the center of our three-way bond, our spiritual journey was the center of our lives. Neither of us could have carried the load if it were not for being secure in Christ. Although our struggle to understand why God was allowing this to happen to us caused us to question our faith at times, it strengthened who we both were in Christ as God's adopted children.

Our personal cancer journey further cemented our marriage. Our worldviews were different, but after we married both Stephen and I marveled at the Bible as the inerrant, inspired, authoritative Word of God, especially in the latter years of Stephen's life. We believed it was God's will for us to be united in marriage to serve him together for a brief time, as we continued to align our wills with his. On October 9, 2011, Stephen experienced the ultimate healing, glorification. His identity in Christ as a child of God was sealed and his eternity with him secured.

Discerning Identity

I now realize the importance of our identity in Christ. In the twenty-first century the institutional church's definition of a Christian is vague; this is largely due to biblical eisegesis, as interpreters read meaning into the Bible that is not there. This is a result of not knowing or believing the Word of God or cherry picking Bible verses to support errant theology. The Bible, complete in itself, is like iron sharpening iron. One part of it helps us to understand another and the fullness of its meaning must not be tampered with.

Ephesians 2:8–10 provides a clear definition: "For by grace you have been saved through faith. And this is not your own doing; it is the gift of God, not a result of works, so that no one may boast. For we are his workmanship, created in Christ Jesus for good works, which God prepared beforehand, that we should walk in them." Verses 8 and 9 talk about salvation coming through faith alone in the grace of God alone through the redemptive work of Christ on the cross and not through our works. This is true, but leaving out verse 10 is taking it out of context, and not what God desires of biblically faithful Christians. Salvation is based on nothing we do—but good works, our fruits, are a result of genuine salvation through Christ. Our identity in him is most important, and how we live flows from that. We reflect whose we are. Our salvation is a gift from God, but it did not come cheaply. Accepting God's gift, and following Christ, will bring a change in character called the new birth, or regeneration. Good works resulting from the love given back to God bear the fruit of salvation and give evidence of rebirth. We become new creations.

In Matthew 7, near the end of the Sermon on the Mount, Jesus speaks of fruit through a parable. He warned his disciples not to accept the teaching of false prophets, whose fruits are only good for the fire (also Luke 6:43–45). Earlier, in Matthew 5:18, Jesus had said that he had not come to abolish the Jewish law but to fulfil it. Jesus's sacrificial death replaced the Israelite animal sacrifice but did not abolish God's laws and commandments; their authority was confirmed for eternity. God's laws teach us what he hates and guide us to live according to his will. The sin of antinomianism, that believers may live as they wish to once they are saved and never need to repent of further sin, contradicts justification by faith through grace. Legalism, belief in salvation by good works and obeying God's laws, is antithetical to salvation through the blood of Christ.

> Beware of false prophets, who come to you in sheep's clothing but inwardly are ravenous wolves. You will recognize them by their fruits. Are grapes gathered from thorn bushes, or figs from thistles? So, every

healthy tree bears good fruit, but the diseased tree
bears bad fruit. A healthy tree cannot bear bad fruit,
nor can a diseased tree bear good fruit. Every tree
that does not bear good fruit is cut down and thrown
into the fire. Thus you will recognize them by their
fruits. (Matthew 7:15–20)

Who we say we are and how we live as children of God is crucial. The
importance of righteousness within God's kingdom is highlighted
at the end of Christ's revelation to John. Revelation 22:14 (KJV)
makes clear that how Christians live mirrors their hearts, and God
is most concerned with the heart; those that do his commandments
are blessed, have the right to the tree of life, and may enter the city
by the gates—the obedient have a legitimate right to eternal life.
Growing into the persons God desires us to be is a lifelong process.
Living how the Bible says we should live is crucial to our impact as
Christians in the world.

IDENTITY SECURED

The glass experience taught me that God loves me and knows me
even though I do not fully know him or myself. He identifies me
by name and knows my every thought, the number of my days, and
who I will become. He was listening to my thoughts in January 2008
just as he does every moment of every day.

There is no identity crisis when we fall in love with God, ponder
him and his ways, reflect upon his Word, contemplating and learning
about who he is, all that he is, and realize all that we are and can
be in, through, and with him. It is imperative to seek to know who
God is and what he desires so that we know him personally. By

honestly confronting who we are, and all that we can become as God's adopted children, we have the choice to be reconciled to his ways, following them as our own, or not. It is a conscious decision to follow Christ, and to be identified by him to God.

Our only true identity is our relationship to God through Jesus. God desires that we sincerely seek him with humble, contrite hearts. He desires a relationship with all of his children. We need only seek to find, ask to be given. There is peace, freedom, and joy when our identity in Christ is secure, for we are only whole when we come to Christ, through sincerely searching after God and studying his Word.

CHAPTER 3

R: RELATIONSHIPS RIGHT

Listen to me, you who pursue righteousness, you who seek the Lord: look to the rock from which you were hewn, and to the quarry from which you were dug. (Isaiah 51:1)

$\mathcal{W}$e are social beings, but, unlike animals, we were created for relationship with God. Relationships in keeping with God's commands and in the right order are essential for his children as they pursue righteousness and holiness. Although I knew that God was supreme, I did not fully understand what being in a relationship with him meant until I understood the truth of his Word. With my sinful nature in check by the Holy Spirit, and my identity as God's child secure through Christ's blood, I discern God's will for my life.

BIRTH AND ANCESTRY

My first relationships were with my parents, siblings, and extended family. I was blessed to have loved and been loved by four grandparents, and two great-grandparents for a brief time. Their love helped me grow into an emotionally healthy person who could love others. It provided me with a strong moral base that was grounded in their Christian upbringing and supported by my own growth as a Christian. I talked with God, whom I could not see or hear, because I understood the passages of the Bible that I heard in church; I felt God's presence with me as a constant companion.

I was gifted with a remarkably strong heritage. My paternal grandfather, William Vokey (1903–1982), can be traced back to Robert Gosse, born June 9, 1723, at Dorset, England, and died in 1794 in Newfoundland. He was a merchant, shipwright, and fisherman married to Catherine Pike, born 1726, died August 9, 1818, who was a descendant of Gilbert Pike, a Peter Easton pirate (perhaps not my greatest heritage). My paternal grandmother, Ethel Gosse (1905–2001), is traced to Robert's older brother, Richard Gosse, born also in Dorset in 1720, and died in 1760 after settling in Back Cove, Spaniard's Bay. Both of my paternal grandparents descended from these two brothers who, seven generations back, can be traced to John Gosse, born about 1522, a bailiff in Bridport, England, in 1558. My family can be traced back fifteen generations on my paternal grandmother's side and fourteen generations on my paternal grandfather's side. Both the Vokeys and Gosses were settlers in the Spaniard's Bay area in the 1700s but the lineage in the Vokey line is not as easy to follow, possibly due to the origin and spelling of that name.

My maternal grandfather, George Edward Earle (1904–1981), the youngest of the four children of William Earle (1871–1940) and Emily Anne (Marshall), born in Spear Harbour, Labrador (1874–1940), cared for his parents and a sister in their homestead in Carbonear until they died. Pop Earle's grandparents, Moses Earle, born in Harbour Grace and died in Carbonear on April 18, 1917, at age seventy-five, and Patience (Marks), married on December 31, 1863, and had ten children. Moses and Patience were among the earliest members of St. James Anglican Church in Carbonear. My grandfather's family, through his cousin Captain Guy Earle, has been traced back to John d'Erlegh (died in 1166), whose son, Sir William d'Erlegh, was chamberlain to Henry II. My grandfather married Mabel Elizabeth Noel (1910–2006), daughter of Benjamin and Mary (Soper) of Freshwater, whose house still stands, in 2016, in Freshwater, just outside Carbonear.

Reading biblical genealogies caused me to become interested in my own ancestry. I enjoyed my grandparents' stories about their deceased relatives but I had difficulty remembering their names and their relationship to me. What fortitude my ancestors showed in leaving England and crossing the Atlantic under horrendous conditions in search of a better life in the colonies. When they landed safely in this rich, but barren, Newfoundland, their faith was intact and their churches were the centers of their communities.

My mother remembers how her family travelled every spring to Petty Harbour, Labrador, so that Pop Earle could fish with his father and brothers. She remembers staying in her Grandfather Earle's house. When my mother was of school age, her mother would no longer take them to Labrador as she did not want her children to miss any school time. Grandmother Earle finished high school and studied nursing, a great feat in her day, but her favorite memories were those on the Labrador cooking for the fishermen and caring for my mother and my aunt.

I am thankful for a Christian heritage that valued education and motivated me to read, study, and explore God's world. My Grandfather Vokey, a quiet, gentle, and knowledgeable man, had only a Grade Four formal education, but his books on Newfoundland and Labrador, the Beothuks, and the fishing and sealing industries caught my eye when I was eight or nine years old, initiating my love of reading about the world. As a child I always wanted to know who, where, why, what, and when (like my own grandchildren), but now I am more comfortable with not knowing or understanding everything.

Learning about my heritage gave me a new respect for Judaism and the genealogical lists recorded in Matthew, Luke, and elsewhere in the Bible. Three sets of fourteen or fifteen generations, back to back (even when generations are omitted), is not a long time, especially as we age. Although we may inadvertently make errors in our family trees, God does not miss a single generation.

FAMILY MATTERS

Throughout my childhood, attending church was a regular Sunday event. Everyone in my family, and everyone in the entire community that I knew, went to one of four denominational churches. My extended family was an important part of my life for the first ten years until we were scattered by the closing of the Bell Island mines. I remember how, when I was perhaps seven to nine years old, at one extended family event, a great-uncle, Uncle Harry, my Grandmother Vokey's brother, asked me a question. "I just want to ask you one question, Marilyn. Do you have to believe in miracles to be a Christian?" I thought a little, before saying, "Yes, you do." There was no other answer to the question when I considered the virgin birth of Jesus and his miraculous resurrection; I knew nothing of modern-day miracles at that time in my life. Although I knew some of the Old Testament stories, I did not believe them to be true like the New Testament miracles. Jesus was familiar to me, as I had heard about him in church and read about him in my Bible story books. Uncle Harry replied, "You got that one right."

From Child to Adult

As I approached adolescence I no longer felt safe. Growing up in the mining town of Wabana/Bell Island, where employment was good at that time, may have provided me with a false sense of security. Our move to a rental property on the outskirts of St. John's in 1962, where my father worked several jobs to support us, caused some apprehension and insecurity in me. We did, however, continue to attend church regularly on Sundays.

For much of my childhood and early adult life I was swayed by those who were well-liked and vocal. I lived life to the fullest, within my means, following the culture. As a teenager I read Hollywood movie-star magazines and popular mystery and romance novels, like most girls my age were reading. I watched the entertaining programs on one of the two television channels available that were, in comparison to today's programs, more in keeping with biblical standards of behavior. I accepted the desires and goals of the world, believing that a good education would bring a good job with enough money to have a nice home, car, good food, and new clothes. In the meantime, it was important to have friends, and a boyfriend, if you were female. As the eldest of six children, there was little time for friends outside of school, homework, and household chores. I knew from talk at school that alcohol, drugs, and sex were often associated with getting together on weekends especially, but they did not dominate my life. The one sexual relationship I had, resulting in teenage marriage, steered my life in what was a much healthier direction than what might have been.

My faith in Jesus and God, no matter how immature, was formed enough that I knew abortion was against God's teaching and not the answer to my unplanned pregnancy at seventeen. Abortion was mentioned twice, by a family member and by a doctor, but it was not an option for me, nor was giving up my child for adoption. This child was part of me and Corb, whom I loved more than anyone and who loved me; we were responsible for our actions. Responsibility was something I learned well, as I had often heard my mother say, "You make your bed hard, you'll have to lie in it." By relying on God, as I had throughout my childhood, although my parents disapproved of my marrying at seventeen, I married Corb and had absolute peace through it all. Corb and I took our marriage vows seriously, and God drew us closer to him and to each other as we regularly attended Corb's church.

In my twenties I lacked self-confidence, relying on Corb to fight my battles, even to return an item to a store if it was less-than-a-straightforward transaction. Although much too brief, our marriage and family life were healthy and loving. God was always in the back of my mind, but not the center as he should have been. We said a prayer over meals and before going to bed, we went to church regularly each Sunday, but we did not study the Bible or discuss the biblical essentials of the Christian faith. In 1983 our lives were catapulted on a totally different trajectory as we began a fierce ten-month cancer battle. Faith and church community were part of our lives but relationship with God was tenuous, at best. Regardless, we trusted God for healing, but it did not come.

After Corb's death, in September 1984, I had to be strong to survive and raise two children as a single, working parent. As I rethought life, its purpose, and faith, I became more spiritually minded and briefly toyed with belief systems outside Christianity, including New Age mysticism. I was angry with God for not healing Corb, and I would have been happy to learn he did not exist, yet the Bible taught that he did. I believed in an always-present transcendent God, but I did not like or understand his ways. I did not always lean on him, but I kept on going to church. As I found out how difficult it was to raise children alone, I cried out more to God for help, and he sent me into the Bible for answers and understanding.

RELATIONSHIP WITH GOD

Healthy relationships take time and energy to make, develop, and keep. This is especially true when they are kept as God intends. How we relate to one another depends on our reasons for and purpose of a relationship, the character and identities of all involved, and God's place in the relationship. I was a church member through baptism and confirmation, but I did not have a clear understanding of what it meant to be in a relationship with God—that was not explained or discussed, not even in church, and therefore not relevant to me. Before I changed churches, when I married Corb, I had been taught about sin and its consequences, especially with respect to Holy Communion. I learned how confession and repentance resulted in forgiveness and reconciliation with God, but I never knew how sin grieved the Holy Spirit and separated us from God. My heart's attitude toward sin and God's Word was not right.

Bible reading was not something I knew that anyone, except my grandmother, did. To me reading was what I did for school homework, or the magazines and novels I read in my leisure time—never the Bible. Living life to the fullest meant taking every opportunity for success and pleasure in this life, not really caring about the next. There was little time for God during the week beyond saying perfunctory meal and bedtime prayers. I do, however, remember talking privately to God many times, especially when I was upset, and crying, which, as a child, seemed often. I looked to God for his love at those times.

During Corb's illness, I went through the first four of Dr.

Elisabeth Kubler-Ross's five stages of death and grief—anger, denial, bargaining, and depression—but I only ever saw Corb exhibit the last one, acceptance. When I asked him one day why he never became angry, he replied, "We wouldn't have gotten angry if we had won the lottery, would we?" This, I felt, was a strange comment, as we had only once bought a lottery ticket. Corb's response was indicative of how he dealt with life. He knew what many Israelites did not, that it is how we deal with circumstances, not the circumstances themselves, that makes the difference. Corb's attitude impacted how he lived and how he died. He dealt admirably with his illness and impending death and he had gone to be with Jesus peacefully. He was not experiencing my pain, the pain of missing him. Even then I knew there were worse things than death, but I came to realize that not knowing God through Jesus is worst of all. The Bible equates death with sleep and Ecclesiastes 9:5 tells us that the dead experience nothing, grief nor sadness. Yet 1 Thessalonians 4:13–14, 2 Corinthians 5:6–8, and Philippians 1:23 assure believers that one day we will be reunited with Jesus. I believed that Corb was with Jesus, but that did not stop me from blaming God for his death.

After Corb died, I realized that even my getting a degree and subsequently teaching was a gift from God, because then I could financially care for us. I would not have had an income if I had not worked, since Corb had only nine years and nine months of government service, three months short of a pension. Although I was thankful for God's bountiful provision, I still was so distraught over his death that I felt that my life was over. Many times I wished it was. Several times I thought of driving over the cliff at Middle Cove or slashing my wrists, but I could not do this to the God who had gifted me with life. I believed that God would forgive me for taking my own life, but I knew that it was not his desire for me to end my life.

Despite my anger with God, I attended a church regularly. Although I felt that God had abandoned me or was punishing me, I could not deny that he existed, but I did not know him well. I loved my children deeply and felt it was important for them to carry on our Christian tradition, know that Jesus was real, and develop deeper relationships with God than their father and I had had. I believed that if God was real and we were united through Jesus we would all be reunited with Corb one day.

Attending a church does not mean that a person has a relationship with God, prays, reads the Bible, or even knows how to love his or her neighbors. When I realized that the church we attended was not biblically faithful, not even from a New Testament perspective, and did not provide any different moral example for my children than the school system did, I prayed for them more, relied less on the church, and found a new church home. I trusted in God, the psalms, and the New Testament rather than in people. Psalm 118:8, the central verse of the Bible, teaches us that it is better to take refuge in the Lord than to trust in man; and I did.

GOD LOVES ME!

For a long time, I was angry that God did not do what I thought was best. My anger was best aimed at God, rather than at people, because he could handle it. For many years after Corb's death I felt a gaping hole running right through me. In 2013, after Stephen died, I sketched my emotions of how I felt after Corb died. I needed to deal with the images in my mind and let it go. Stephen's death did not leave a gaping hole; instead, I experienced the calm and peace I believe that both Stephen and Corb had when they died.

All life experiences leave scars. We only need look at the scars on our bodies from early childhood to realize this, although the wounds have long since healed and the memories dimmed. In 2011, after Stephen's death, because my relationship with God was much stronger, I reacted quite differently than I had in 1984 to Corb's death, although the scars of pain and growth were still there.

Sometime after Corb's death my Grandmother Vokey gave me a keychain with "God Loves Me!" engraved on it. I always treasured her gifts, but I wanted nothing to do with that keychain. I am surprised that I did not throw it away. I could not understand how a God who loved me could break my heart by allowing my husband to die and leave me a widow at thirty-one. I refused to believe that he loved me, but I knew that he was real and that he listened to me. As I called out for answers, reading parts of the Bible, especially Psalms, Proverbs, and the New Testament epistles, God heard my cries and had mercy on me.

I eventually began to enjoy life again. I determined that I would be content in the time that I had left rather than wallow in self-pity and be miserable. By this time, I knew that I knew the God of the Bible through Jesus, and I was beginning to understand the difference among the three persons of the Trinity. I soon felt I was never alone and that with God all things are possible. Through the years that I had been indifferent to him, God was patiently loving me and breathing new life into me through the Holy Spirit, as I read and understood his Word more. I still did not totally trust God or place his will before mine, but I had learned that "what is right is not always popular, and what is popular is not always right," to quote Albert Einstein. Proverbs 14:12 reminds us that the way which seems right to man often is the way to death. My way for many years was spiritually unhealthy. Spiritual health came only when I reconciled my faith in God to his Word and trusted him.

With much prayer, Bible reading, and the healing touch of the

Holy Spirit, God mended my broken heart. I put one foot in front of the other and, with time, I felt like a new person. Much later, having remarried, studied theology, experienced the glass heart, and been widowed a second time, in early 2013 I was happy when I found the keychain, as it reminded me of where I once had been in my Christian walk and how far God had brought me.

Grandmother Vokey had gifted me with the keychain at a time when I was at the depths of grief. I think it was her way of telling me that God had not abandoned me. Strangely, I began to understand what it meant for God to love me. I applied myself to understanding God, as in Ecclesiastes 1:13. I learned that life for many is difficult and what some who appear to be happy deem important is useless, vanity, and a striving after the wind. For the first time I really knew what it meant to be in a loving relationship with God. I began to trust that God did know best.

Everything can seem meaningless, especially after searing loss, but of all that separates us from God's love, the sin of pride is perhaps the worst. People go to almost any length to prove that they can make it on their own. When I ponder the years after Corb's death, I realize my own pride. I did not want to depend on anyone, including the God who created me. In addition to being angry with him and ignoring him, I remained stubborn until I allowed him to comfort me through his Word in the mid- to late 1980s. In 2005 God used Stephen and my love of learning to get me to further explore the Bible through theological study. After Stephen's death I obeyed God's command to study the Old Testament. God used my critical thinking and reasoning abilities to question and seek and search, as he beckoned me to come closer to him.

NAMES MATTER

I know now what I did not understand when my grandmother had given me that keychain. She herself was familiar with grief because she had buried her first child, her only daughter, Elsie Olive, who had died at the age of ten of diabetes. As a child I was told not to eat too much of certain foods as I might get diabetes. The first girl born in the family after Olive's death, I was named after her. It was an honor to have her name, but I was relieved that it was only my middle name. Olive sounded old-fashioned to me. I was born with an arteriovenous fistula on my forehead, visible even with a bang, and I did not want any extra negative attention that an old-fashioned name would bring.

Olive trees in Gethsemane, October 15, 2015

Although I have carried Olive's name all my life, I finally appreciate it, for I am like a green olive tree, trusting in God's steadfast love forever. In Israel I learned that olives, one of seven essential foods delineated for the Hebrews in the Old Testament (two grains and five fruits), represent not only a valuable source of food, medicine, and beauty and oil products but they also link the biblical Promised Land to modern-day Israel. I realize how precious the name *Olive* is. Some olive trees in the Garden of Gethsemane may be from Christ's day, as such trees have lived for over a thousand years. Olive trees, beautiful, strong, and fertile, are symbols of hope, happiness, wisdom, and peace.

I thank God for my grandmother, her daughter, and her name, and I pray for forgiveness for my selfishness, stubborn pride, and hard-heartedness at that time. I have a new appreciation for the way God weaves all of life's intricacies together to make us unique, gently chastising us and molding us into who he wants us to be. I visualize the ancient olive trees of Gethsemane, each comprised of numerous branches woven together to create one strong huge trunk. Each one is majestic, especially when laden with ripe olives.

God binds all Christians together in his truth and love. It stretches my imagination to think of all that is happening at any second in the universe and of all of the strands that connect us through Jesus's blood and the truth of God's Word. Scientists are learning so much about the vast scope of the world we live in, but if they are oblivious to God, what is most important can be lost. God, however, is oblivious to nothing, and he works everything together for the good of those who love him. He uses everything to work together his perfect plan for humanity.

At one of my granddaughter's baptisms I remarked on the strong, beautiful name she was given; she was named for the mothers of Jesus and John the Baptist. When my daughter asked me for a middle name choice for my youngest granddaughter, I gave her a derivative of my middle name, to remember my grandmother and her daughter. Olivia sounded more modern than Olive. I wish now that I had used Olive and been faithful to my grandmother and my heritage, but that was before I visited Israel and God began the deepest reworking of my heart. I realize now that a good name is far better than precious ointment. It is balm for the soul. I understand how the day of death for a believer is better than the day of birth: on that day we will see Jesus. My grandmother knew that she would be with Jesus and Olive when she died in 2001.

So much is lost in a generation if it does not learn from and guard its Christian heritage. For me that heritage was built on faith, steeped in God's Word, and passed down with love. The most important name of all—to me and to many of my ancestors—is God: Father, Son, and Holy Spirit. He is the source of all life.

PERSONAL RELATIONSHIP WITH GOD

God's desire for a personal relationship with those created in his image has remained the same since humans were first created. The choice to accept Jesus has always been ours. Although God created us to relate with one another so closely that we would form family units and have children and grandchildren, his primary desire is for us to have a relationship with him.

The *shema* of Deuteronomy 6:4–9 directed Israel to love the Lord their God with all of their heart, soul, and strength. The Israelites were to live the shema, proclaiming it, teaching it diligently to their children, and talking about God and his Word regularly in their homes. The New Testament command to Christians is no less. The first half of Jesus's commandment is for us to love God with all of our heart, soul, mind, and strength and be in relationship with him (Matthew 22:37). I was familiar with the shema, as I had heard it regularly as part of our weekly Anglican liturgy. I knew I was to love God fully with body and soul. Loving God before all others is difficult, but if I had difficulty understanding it, it was because I had not listened well or not given it enough thought or prayer. It was taught correctly to me in church as a young child and I had appropriate role models in parents, grandparents, and extended family.

Our first love must be for God (Luke 14:26); by comparison, we must hate all family members—parents, spouse, children, siblings, and ourselves. The Greek word used here for hate means to detest or despise. When we understand that in this verse the word *hate* is a comparative term used to emphasize commitment to God before all others, we see that no one should hate another. Nothing or no one should come between us and God. He made us for himself. All other love and relationships is based on this full, loving relationship with God the Father.

All other relationships can only reach their potential if our relationship with God comes first and is strong, vibrant, and healthy. This sets the bar very high in terms of all other relationships. God desires a loving, personal relationship with us. He desires that we model all of our human relationships on our relationship with him, which is impossible in our own strength. It is through God's grace alone and in the power of the Holy Spirit that we are able to be as faithful as it is possible to be, humanly speaking.

I was in my mid- to late thirties when I realized what Luke 14:26 meant and what it meant to be saved. By that time, I knew God as Father and realized I had been a disobedient child; I was living as if there was no relational, immanent God. If I was God's child and part of his family, that would impact the way I was living.

I felt guilty when I sinned but not enough to change my selfish ways. Throughout my childhood, teens, and early adulthood, my relationship with God had matured, but it was not my primary relationship. My love for God did not come before Corb, my children, or my will.

Before my trip to Japan in 1995 and meeting Stephen in 1996, I had made God Lord of my life. But it had taken approximately a decade for me to develop a reverential awe of God and realize that I must obey him. Having traded in romance novels and other fiction for motivational literature, including positive-thinking books, in the mid-1980s, I began to search seriously for the meaning of my existence. Over several years and after reaching rock bottom a second time, I had gone from reading New Age spirituality to crying out the Psalms and Proverbs, watching biblically grounded television programs, and reading Christian books and magazines.

When I consider my spiritual growth at this time, I credit my early Christian heritage. Instead of plunging deep into the New Age or Eastern mysticism, I returned to my Christian roots. Although I had been going through the motions of praying, confessing, and repenting of all I had done, my heart was not right, because I kept living the same old way. But God was lifting me out of the darkness into the light of his Word through the power of the Holy Spirit.

I realized I was God's child not only because he created me and loved me beyond measure but because he had adopted me fully into his family. He desired for me to be his daughter and heir of all that he offers, not to be a slave of this world. I see now how during those years that I was living a prosperous life I was also a slave to the world and what it valued. I had tried to fill the void created by Corb's death with material things and events—worldly things had come between me and my relationship with God.

> I mean that the heir, as long as he is a child, is no different from a slave, though he is the owner of everything, but he is under guardians and managers until the date set by his father. In the same way we also, when we were children, were enslaved to the elementary principles of the world. But when the fullness of time had come, God sent forth his Son, born of woman, born under the law, to redeem those who were under the law, so that we might receive adoption as sons. And because you are sons, God has sent the Spirit of his Son into our hearts, crying, "Abba! Father!" So you are no longer a slave but a son, and if a son, then an heir through God. (Galatians 4:1–7)

Those things that had caused me to waver in my faith for so long eventually lost their grip as I saw their futility and shallowness. The Holy Spirit empowered me to commit fully to God as his child should. His hand was always upon me to comfort, protect, teach, and guide me along his narrow path. I heeded God's voice through the Bible as he taught and healed me. The once-loose connection between God and me became a permanent bond, a binding covenant, as I realized I was his child through Christ, and I wanted and needed him. There was much I did not understand, but my spiritual growth exponentially outweighed my own efforts to be a good Christian.

LEARNING TO BE HIS CHILD

God's expectation of my relationship with him today is the same as it was for Noah, Abraham, Josiah, or Paul in their day. God's standards and requirements for relating with him have not changed. From the time of Moses, over three thousand years ago, God commanded that his ways be taught to his people. Jesus, obedient to God to the point of death, knew the Old Testament far better than the scribes and Pharisees of his day. Christians are commanded to be obedient to God, to the point of death if necessary, and to study his Word.

God desires that nothing come between him and us, including our wills. We are to worship God only, love him first of all, and regularly commune with him. I had learned to put God first in my life, but I had difficulty discerning his will for my life, and at times had difficulty accepting his will over mine. I felt that I knew what was best regarding my life, and it did not include ordained ministry or believing the Old Testament. My spiritual battles over God's command to study the Old Testament and his will for my life decreased after Stephen's death but were not fully resolved until the spring of 2014. Learning full obedience is never easy.

I did not understood wholeness of relationship with God until I gave up mere lip service to respecting his Word and took seriously his command to read and study it—all of it. Bit by bit from the end of 2011 to 2014 I submitted to God's will, which included reading the Bible from cover to cover twice, taking the Old Testament Exegetical study tour to Israel in 2014, and doing intensive Bible study. Through it all God illuminated his Word, so that with new eyes and ears and a softened heart, I saw and understood as if for the first time. God replaced my self-centeredness and erroneous theology with his truth.

Through the Holy Spirit God helped me to see things his way as I digested his Word and listened to him, not the world. Visiting Israel was helpful, but it did not replace obediently reading and studying God's Word. I still do not understand many parts of the Bible, but I know that no person will ever understand it fully. It will remain mystery.

Unknowingly I had set boundaries on God. Everything was acceptable as long as he did not override my will to what I could see as being logical, rational, acceptable, and completely comfortable, in worldly terms. But God is not limited or concerned by what irrational humanity, including me, thinks. I had to forget about trying to understand everything, like creation, why God commanded the Israelites to kill and be separate, how Jesus will return, or why only some are healed. Greater clarity, though, does come the more I pray, read, and study the Bible.

Some say God is dead, some say he never existed, and some believe that a relationship with him is a crutch. Life without God is life without truth, for God *is* truth. Jesus and the Holy Spirit have empowered me and enriched my life far more than the things of the world, more than all of the money, power, fame, sex, and control, which never can satisfy. God makes life worth living. I do not desire to change my life in any way and would not want to live without God as Lord of it. There is nothing or no one on earth I desire more than God. My physical body and my mind will fail, but my spirit will live forever. God, the strength of my heart, mind, and will, sustains me.

FATHER AND CHILD

Both Judaism and Christianity speak of God as Father. God is not referred to as Father as often in the Old Testament as he is in the New, but he is referred to as Father in at least Deuteronomy 32:6; Psalms 68:5, 89:26, 103:13 and Malachi 2:10. Only the God of the Bible claims to be God, the Father. He is my Father; I am his child. I know that if I, who am evil, know how to give good gifts to my children and grandchildren, how much more will my heavenly Father give good things to me and to all who ask him. I gave my children too much and was strict with them, but I provided them with love, sound biblical teaching, and wise Christian counsel. God has gifted them, as he has gifted all people, with wills of their own to make their own choices.

Our relationships with our parents affect how we conceptualize God as Father. My children knew and loved their father, but from ages thirteen and seven they were raised by a single mother. Although faith and an understanding of the Bible helped me to love God, my children may have felt distant from him and blamed him for their father's death. The privilege of having two parents pales in comparison to knowing that I am a child of God and that I have a heavenly Father who loves me. I always took seriously the command to honor and obey my parents, although I fell short many times. Much later I realized that life lived for God's glory is contingent on obeying this commandment.

OBEDIENCE AND DISCIPLINE

I loved my father despite his strict discipline. Growing up at a time where a stiff upper lip was expected and showing affection seen as a weakness, my father demonstrated his love just as easily as he showed his dissatisfaction through physical punishment. I am thankful that he loved me enough to discipline me.

> "My son, do not regard lightly the discipline of the Lord, nor be weary when reproved by him. For the Lord disciplines the one he loves, and chastises every son whom he receives." It is for discipline that you have to endure. God is treating you as sons. For what son is there whom his father does not discipline? If you are left without discipline, in which all have

> participated, then you are illegitimate children and
> not sons. Besides this, we have had earthly fathers
> who disciplined us and we respected them. Shall we
> not much more be subject to the Father of spirits
> and live? For they disciplined us for a short time
> as it seemed best to them, but he disciplines us for
> our good, that we may share his holiness. For the
> moment all discipline seems painful rather than
> pleasant, but later it yields the peaceful fruit of
> righteousness to those who have been trained by it.
> (Hebrews 12:5–11)

My father served in the Army reserve during some summer months, and my siblings and I laughed and joked about the "swagger," a wooden stick covered in leather that I thought was related to his part-time job. I can remember seeing the stick when it was fully covered in leather as well as bare. I thought that the leather had worn off because the stick hit us, me especially, so much, but I realize now that that was a child's perception.

In my later years, with teenage children of my own, I realized the value of discipline. I chastised my children with lectures, gave them rewards for good behavior, and doled out negative consequences for poor behavior and disobedience. The one time that I disciplined my daughter by spanking her bottom I had to go to my bedroom afterwards to cry. There was a similar incident with my son, but he believed the only physical punishment he received was from his father. The two times I remember physically disciplining my children hurt me more than it hurt them.

The importance of discipline was highlighted as I was teaching a Grade Six class. We were discussing rights and responsibilities and how our lives change as we age and take on more responsibility.

One boy expressed concern that his parents always wanted to know where he was going and what he was doing with his friends. He was displeased about being disciplined by losing his allowance and his favorite television show, and possibly being spanked. As he finished speaking, one girl retorted, "Well, at least you know your parents care about you. My mother doesn't care where I am or who I'm with." This comment came from a girl who several times that year dressed her younger sister and brought her to school, even though her mother may not have come home the night before. This beautiful eleven-year-old girl could connect discipline and love. Children can understand how fair and equitable discipline enforced by parents or teachers show that they genuinely care for them.

I, too, must obey God's laws and listen to his voice before I can relate to others as he commands. We must constantly and regularly read God's Word to be open to his prompting to love, be patient, and treat others the way he desires us to. The Holy Spirit will empower us to act when we are obedient to God's will and his time. Although obedience and discipline are complicated topics, we should not worry about unfairness or withheld discipline from God; he is the faultless disciplinarian, knowing what each of us requires before we need it. Obeying God to the point of understanding and appreciating his ways, even his discipline, takes careful study of his Word, and much prayer.

RELATIONSHIPS GOD'S WAY

During the second half of my life I am learning what it means to be in the world and not of it, because of God's love for me. Through regular Bible reading and meditation and prayer, and with the guidance of the Holy Spirit, I rely on my heavenly Father. I rejoice that he made himself known to me through Jesus, and that he insisted on my obedience. I now have remarkable peace, a peace that does surpass all human understanding.

All family relationships are secondary to my relationship with God. Relationships with other Bible-believing Christians, many of whom do not believe exactly as I believe, but we agree on biblical essentials, are pivotal to keeping my faith and trust in God true and sharp as we all work toward a more intimate relationship with him through reading the Bible, worship, fellowship with other Christians, and prayer. I am overjoyed to be God's daughter and part of his family. Because of it, my life with my family and others has been enriched, despite the tension that ensues when some disagree with my beliefs and values. Only striving to meet God's standard matters. To have the proper and right relationship with God, my heart had to be ready and my selfish will broken. I had to learn how much sin hurts God and grieves the Holy Spirit.

CHAPTER 4

C: CHILDLIKE TRUST

Truly, I say to you, whoever does not receive the kingdom of God like a child shall not enter in. (Mark 10:15)

*O*f the ways that I understand my relationship with God, it is the parent-child bond, that intimate, familial way of connecting with him, which resonates with me most. My faith in God as Father causes me to approach him as a little child who totally depends on and trusts her father whom she knows loves her. My childlike faith has grown into a complete, all-sufficient trust in God and commitment to his will that is not childish but firmly rooted in his Word.

IN HIS IMAGE

All humans are made in God's image. The first humans that God breathed into being were fully relational with him spiritually, until sin entered their world. Between sin's entrance and Pentecost, God imbued his chosen ones with the ability to know him but, after Pentecost, the Holy Spirit indwelt all who trusted Jesus for salvation. Although God created all humans in his image, only those born again have God's Spirit indwelling them and are his adopted children.

Our children resemble us physically, emotionally, and in other ways, but they may not resemble us spiritually. Although as parents we provide what we think is spiritually sound, they may not choose to follow God's way, because salvation is the act of a person's will. It is not inborn, infused, caught, taught, passed on, or earned through works, but is an individual, conscientious decision to accept God's free gift of salvation through Jesus.

Most of my life I accepted the New Testament with a childlike faith, but I did not understand much of it. I was taught that most of the Old Testament was myth and hyperbole. Over the past decade by actually reading, studying, and evaluating the Bible and comparing it to what critics have written about it, I find that there is sufficient proof in it alone to trust God and his Word. My faith, however, leads me to accept everything God revealed in the Bible as true, although I do not know or understand how all of it is so.

The two children I gave birth to originate biologically from me and their father. They were the consequences of human actions, but they are also made in God's image. As adults, they are responsible for their own decisions and have responsibility for their children, also made in God's image, but only God knows if my children and grandchildren are his children and resemble him spiritually. Understanding what being created in God's image means is difficult even when we consult his Word, but it is impossible without it. We know we are not in God's image in a physical sense, because he is Spirit. We know that even those who say they do not believe in Jesus or in God are still made in his image. Those in God's image in Christ have the Holy Spirit indwelling them and they reflect God's character and obey him because they have become new creations.

Before I studied the Bible, I did not understand the full significance of parenting. My children reflect my character, and their father's, but they were as much our spiritual responsibility as they were our physical responsibility. I have repented and been forgiven for taking insufficient spiritual responsibility for my children, for giving the church more responsibility than I allowed the educational system responsibility for their learning. The consequences of an improper relationship with God can be severe and may last forever.

My ignorance of God's Word may have provided an excuse for me in the past, but it does so no longer. There is no excuse for not reading and knowing it. Just as it is my civil responsibility to know the laws of the road and of the land, it is even more so my Christian responsibility to know God, his ways, and his laws if I say that he is my God. If I believe Jesus is my Lord and the way to God, I will. The Bible repeatedly and clearly delineates how parents are to raise their children. I now know, as God's child, the magnitude of parental (and grandparenting) roles, and of leadership roles in the church.

Through immature faith I began to spiritually grow as a Christian. Slowly I began to accept God's will for my life. In my own strength, I can do little but, by his Word and through the indwelling Holy Spirit, I am beginning to understand who God is. We can only be Christ-like when we are God's children. That means accepting God as Father and Jesus as Savior with a childlike faith that develops into our trusting God with all of our minds, hearts, spirits, and wills.

CHILDHOOD FAITH

I remember being in church as a young child and smelling the wood as I sat on the kneeler. My siblings and I remained in church with our parents for the morning service and attended Sunday school in the afternoon. We did not complain that we had to go to church in the afternoon—we just went. Being brought up to know that there was a God was as important as going to school. In the late 1950s in my community parents usually brought their children to church and were part of a church family.

I remember singing hymns in church, especially those my grandmother sang to me—"Tell Me the Stories of Jesus," "Can a Little Child Like Me," "Jesus Bids Us Shine," "All Things Bright and Beautiful," "Jesus Loves Me," and "God Sees the Little Sparrow Fall"—hymns with solid theology and solace, hymns that taught us about God. When I was older, I took the hymn book and sang the hymns through, always beginning with number one, "Holy, Holy, Holy, Lord God Almighty. Early in the morning our song shall rise to thee." I loved that hymn. When my grandmother talked and sang about him, the words and her voice comforted me.

The first time I prayed to God I knew he heard me. I was praying the Lord's Prayer on my knees beside my bed. After that, whether praying the Lord's Prayer or petitioning him with a list of needs, by my bed, behind the rocking chair, or in the closet, talking to God was a pleasant pastime. I knew God loved me, listened to me, and knew everything I did or thought about. Even when I was a preschooler, God soothed my aching heart, as did the songs I heard and sang.

Lyrics and music are powerful forces in forming who we are. The hymns that I loved as a child were replaced with more modern hymns and choruses, some paraphrases of the Bible. These helped deepen my faith. "Create in Me a Clean Heart, O God" helped me call out to God for cleansing and refining as David, with his heart patterned after God's heart, did millennia ago. I wanted to please God even more than please my father; I knew that God was far more important than my father. Psalm 51:10–12 speaks to my heart as I cry out to God, asking him to renew my spirit and not cast me from his presence or take his Spirit from me. The Lord restores me with joy when I sing to him. My two young granddaughters love listening to, and easily memorize, lyrics to secular music. Because lyrics are powerful teaching tools, and we must guard what our children see, hear, and sing, I introduced them to Christian children's music.

I have experienced the faith of a child, and it is precious. When I talk with my grandchildren about God, I sense their innocence as they ask what God is like. Based on their questions and comments, I feel their belief in a God they cannot see, who loves them and created them. Children trust those who love them, without fear, as most have not yet learned the extent of human depravity and hence their need for guidance and protection. God desires us to intuitively trust him as young children do.

Children pray; with eyes closed and heads bowed, my grandchildren concentrate on my words when I pray. They ask questions when they do not understand. I have heard them ask for prayer for mommy or daddy, who is sick, usually only with a sniffle, for a family member or friend who, in their minds, they sense may be in trouble. I know God hears their words and knows their hearts. When I ask my grandchildren to pray with me for someone they do not know, they give their full attention. I understand why Jesus told the apostles to let the little children come to him and why he taught that we were to have faith like theirs: young, innocent children are close to God's heart.

Costly Prosperity

Church life played a pivotal role in my upbringing. However, I do not see it playing much of a role in many families here in Newfoundland today; Sundays are like any other day for the majority of the population, and few attend the ever-declining numbers of churches. This is largely because few value faith in an unseen God whom they feel is judgmental. To some, religion is oppressive and irrelevant.

This erosion in Christian faith happened subtly, but quickly, as a result of higher education, economic growth, prosperity, easy access to alcohol and drugs, and the woes within specific denominations and church-run institutions.

We have limited faith in our governments, our military, education and health systems, and child care, and more faith in our own abilities, but there is little faith in God or his Word. We know better than the God of the Bible, so we think. We are consumed with information: reading and listening, researching and studying, googling and chatting, but little of it is based on biblical truth. Throughout history the Bible ignited the desire to learn, to read, and to know more about God. Today it is rarely read or consulted. If it is read, in some churches, the reading follows stringent guidelines. Some, even in churches, work hard to rewrite, reinterpret, and even ban God's Word.

We live in a world of "me." We love entertainment, sports, reading, and listening to music. We joke about favorite toys—cars, motorcycles, snowmobiles, sports equipment, electronic gadgets, and designer watches, to name a few. We desire and revel in brand-name shoes, the latest craze in jewelry, designer jeans, and the latest movies and novels. We have time for leisure activities but no time for God. Our habits, which our children see and model, will determine our legacy and their future.

Even though we may have been baptized into a church, confirmed, or even immersed in water, few have time for God or attending church, although we make time for recreation, rest, shopping, and socializing. We desire happiness for ourselves, our children, and our grandchildren. Happiness may include contentment, but, no matter the definition, it is fleeting: it is whatever you desire it to be. One person's happiness can destroy another's. "I want to be happy" is a statement not easily defined, or realized. Wanting to be loved seems easier to define but not always easy to achieve. Being happy and loved are best defined in spiritual terms, but spiritual concepts are foreign to many. Their eyes and ears are closed and their hearts hardened to the God who made them. They believe that everyone will eventually end up in heaven, if there is one, as a loving God, if he created a hell, would not relegate anyone to it.

Sin, righteousness, holiness, and repentance have become archaic, draconian concepts even for churches who use such terminology in their liturgies. When these concepts are taught, often it is according to church doctrine and tradition, not God's standard, the Bible. Sometimes there is so much inconsistency, even within a single church, that the right hand does not seem to know what the left is doing within what is supposedly the one body. There is much confusion in the church, of which God is not the author.

The Narrow Gate

Jesus told us that only the narrow gate leads to life. The wide gate leads to destruction. The Bible says that as we get closer to the time of Jesus's second coming more people will try to enter God's kingdom through the wide gate. When Jesus proclaimed the great commission, mandating his followers to spread the good news of the gospel, so that people will find the narrow gate, he taught us to trust God's Word. Many inspiring stories of the spread of the gospel intrigue me, but Abraham Ulrikab's story, featured February 11, 2016, in a Canadian Broadcasting Corporation (CBC) documentary, is especially poignant.

Abraham Ulrikab's Story

Newfoundland and Labrador, Canada's tenth province, includes Newfoundland, an island, and Labrador, part of the mainland of Canada. Labrador comprises 73 percent of our land mass but only 8 percent of our population, including the Northern Inuit, Southern Inuit-Metis, and Innu. The first time I visited Labrador and spoke with Aboriginal people was in 1969 as a Grade Eleven student on a school trip to Happy Valley-Goose Bay for their first winter carnival.

As a Grade Four teacher in the 1983/1984 school year I befriended Rev. Bill Peacock, the last British Moravian superintendent in Labrador, and his wife, Doris, after Rev. Peacock visited my class to talk about Inuit customs and traditions relative to his Labrador experience. I first learned of the Moravians in Labrador as a Grade Five student. The picture in my textbook of the church band playing on the roof of the Moravian church in Nain is still vivid in my mind. Over the ensuing months Corb and I, with our children, visited with the Peacocks. Knowing the Peacocks' love for the people of Labrador heightened my interest in the Moravians. While I was writing this book, talking with my mother about her trips to Labrador reignited my interest in the Moravian and Anglican presence there. The Anglican church in Battle Harbour was named St. James, as her Carbonear home church was, but it was the Moravians, in Labrador since 1771, who brought the gospel to most natives by the mid-1800s.

The plight of eight Labrador Inuit, as told by CBC, was based on Abraham Ulrikab's diary, one of the earliest known Inuit autobiographies. In August 1880 Abraham (January 29, 1845–January 13, 1881), his wife, two young daughters, a single man, along with another man, his wife, and teen daughter, travelled willingly with John Jacobsen to Europe to be displayed in a zoo. The money they would receive was to pay debts and allow them to see Europe. Soon after arriving in Germany all of them became homesick and realized that they had made a mistake in leaving Labrador. Abraham, his family, and the single man were Christians. Their faith was sustained by morning and evening prayers, singing from a hymn book, and reading and studying Abraham's Bible. Visits to, and by, German Moravian brethren encouraged them. Abraham's and his family's steadfast, childlike trust in God upheld them in the harshest of realities. Their faith is not only a testimony to what God does in us, through us, and with us, but also what he does as part of his grand master plan. Despite eventually being vaccinated, all eight died of smallpox before the middle of January 1881. Their remains, housed in Paris and Berlin, have yet to be repatriated to their land, but Abraham's story testifies to how faith in God sustains all those who love him.

Abraham read and wrote Inuktitut, knew a little English and a few German words, and could play the violin, clarinet, and guitar, all the legacy of the Moravian missionaries. Abraham's diary is a poignant account of immovable, childlike faith. His writing portrayed his love for God and a godly love and respect for others, even those who placed his group on ethnographic display for the entertainment and edification of the curious. Abraham's diary is the only known written work describing some of what happened to approximately thirty-five thousand human specimens in Carl Hagenbeck's exhibitions from the mid-1800s to 1958, but it is a glowing testament of God's love and provision for his people and our eternal hope through Jesus.

Learning about Abraham, his family, and the four other Inuit from Labrador reminded me of my family's precious time with the Peacocks in the last months of both Corb's and Rev. Peacock's lives. As I researched Abraham's story, I learned more about the dedication of the Moravian missionaries and their impact on individuals and communities on several continents—lasting treasure of the narrow gate.

CURIOSITY, CREATIVITY, AND CRITICAL THINKING

As children grow and socialize, they are bombarded by a multitude of influences. Even those who are saved can be swayed by the devil into breaking God's commandments. All children require the love and direction of wise and godly parents to ensure their physical and spiritual well-being. Talking and learning about God and his ways at home, modelled by Christian parents and other family members, help children discern the difference between good and evil, so that they may do what is right in God's eyes. The Bible teaches the importance of wise counsel, godly instruction, and prayer to ensure children's healthy spiritual growth. It admonishes parents to teach their children of God's truth and his love.

Because the devil and his army counterfeit all gifts, especially those of creativity and curiosity, the church is responsible for guarding the truth of God's Word. Curiosity needs to be encouraged, but guided, so that children can learn God's truths themselves by exploring what God says in the Bible. Their questions must be encouraged and our answers wise and godly. When churches do not teach the truth of God's Word and people no longer read it, they are susceptible to everything the devil throws at them. Unsaved church members too fall prey to false teaching and the devil's lies. When they are steeped in God's Word, believers' hearts are quickened by the Holy Spirit to think critically and discern.

Saying that the Bible is a myth or hyperbole is tied to the same element that is stifling natural curiosity, creativity, and critical thinking. Watching people in malls or theaters, we see homogenization in colors and styles of clothing, hairstyles, and even the way people move. Biblical thinking, which runs counter to so-called enlightened, Western thought, is often suppressed. Being curious or critical of the culture is greatly discouraged. The Bible teaches us to be good citizens, but healthy skepticism, or considering other hypotheses, which should be encouraged, often are not. The church seems to be part of the agenda to make everyone fit within culturally defined boundaries. Unidirectional thinking benefits no one, not science, democracy, or the church.

Critically observing what we read, watch, and listen to in our leisure time may result in our realizing just how little evaluation and discernment actually is taking place, especially in light of God's Word and how far from God we are. Often we trust people when it is not wise to do so, as Abraham Ulrikab did. His desire to pay his debts while seeing Europe cost his family their lives, but it did not take their souls. When we trust God as both the patriarch Abraham and Abraham Ulrikab did, we do not need to worry or fear; we are in God's capable, loving hands, our eternity is secure, and we will love others as God requires.

I thought that what I read and the programs I watched in my youth were entertaining and harmless. After studying the Bible, however, I realize that, while entertaining on the surface, a portion of these frivolous activities is harmful. Some books I read and some television programs I watched caused me to believe that wishes, spells, and magic were normal child's play; but, according to the Bible, they are harmful. I wonder also if some classical and popular children's literature, although well-written and entertaining, may have a darker meaning. We need wise teaching to help children discern between fiction and non-fiction, fantasy and reality, truth and lies.

Popular culture helps form and normalize the thinking of most people. Wishing upon a star, making a wish while blowing out birthday candles, striking a yoga pose, or casting a circle may seem innocent, but these seemingly benign culturally ingrained activities may lead to further erosion of Christian faith and impact one's eternal salvation if children are not instructed as God commands them to be instructed. Our society has become desensitized to what is of God; this is largely due to biblical illiteracy. People can seem overly critical, but they may not show any discernment about those things the Bible admonishes us to abstain from. Even when we are God's children, like Abraham Ulrikab, worldly influences and lures beckon us and our children away. Saying a prayer before a meal in a restaurant is not a contested issue until children realize that other people are watching. God desires our hearts to be open and sincere. He knows when those who come to him have faith in and trust him as a little child. God knew what would become of Abraham Ulrikab, just as he knew what the patriarch Abraham would do.

BIRTH AND REBIRTH

At university I studied pre-med my first year. I was interested in psychiatry but not in the hard work associated with studying chemistry. Neither God nor my studies was my first love at that time. At the end of the academic year I switched to education, completing my degree quickly so that I could teach, support us, and raise our son, while Corb finished the last two years of his business degree. We were later gifted with a daughter, because Corb wanted other children. I am so grateful that he did, because I did not.

In September 2007, I was delighted when Carolyn asked me if I would be her backup coach in the delivery room. The delivery was difficult. I was happy to be there, not only to coach her through and support her but, more importantly, to pray. Her beautiful daughter was a treasure for Stephen and me, and continues to bless me. We took care of Maria for much of her second year as Carolyn returned to teaching. Our moving houses to be closer to them was why I used a wine glass to cut out raisin buns in January 2008. In August 2010, although Stephen's health had deteriorated, I was present for the birth of Carolyn's second child, but my heart was heavy due to his precarious health. The second delivery was a breeze. The staff said Carolyn could easily be a poster child for the delivery room. Mya delights me just as Maria and my other grandchildren do. I rejoice, as God does, in their individuality.

Being present for the deliveries of two of my granddaughters, coaching and praying my daughter through their births, and cutting their umbilical cords, was the greatest gift Carolyn could have given me. The gifts of my own two children and being present for the birth of two granddaughters have helped me understand the heart of God. I believe that he rejoices in our births and celebrates our full potential, especially when we live for him and in his will, more than we delight in the births of our own children.

The Bible tells us that we must be born again if we are to enter the kingdom of God. The New Testament describes those who are converted through Jesus as becoming new creatures through him and the Holy Spirit, who indwells all who are born again. Our old natures die as we are reborn as children of God. The Old and New Testaments refer to circumcision of the heart, the change that occurs on rebirth. Being reborn as children of God can be a difficult process, just as childbirth is, but the Holy Spirit eases the pain, comforting, guiding, encouraging, and reassuring all those who are being reborn.

PART OF THE FAMILY

To be a child of God means that I am a part of the family of God. Jesus said, "Let the little children come to me and do not hinder them, for to such belongs the kingdom of heaven" (Matthew 19:14; see also Luke 18:16). God's family includes all who believe Jesus is the Christ. As young children, my siblings, friends, and I romanticized adoption: adopted children were fortunate, we thought—they were purposely chosen and given their own way. Adoption as God's children is infinitely more precious.

Knowing my ancestry became important when I began an intense study of the Old Testament. As I studied the kings of Israel and Judah and learned how some followed God, while others did what they wanted, I could see similarities with my own generational lines—some followed God, others did not. Trying to do what is right and good in the eyes of God does not necessarily mean that our parents and grandparents did or that our own children and grandchildren will even want a relationship with God. It does not mean that our family will respect our right to choose Jesus as Master of our lives and God's Word as ultimate truth.

As I studied the Bible, I wanted to learn what it meant to be part of the family of God. The New Testament epistles taught about the false doctrines being disseminated to the early church, but these epistles also apply to us today. Godly discernment is required so that believers are not taken in by these false teachings. Recognizing other members of God's family has nothing to do with judgment but everything to do with the wisdom given to us by a loving Father who desires that his truth not be polluted.

TRUSTING GOD AS HIS CHILD

Believers are to seek first God's kingdom. I have been doing that, on and off, all of my life. Faithfulness in reading and studying the entire Bible was missing until 2011; trusting God completely came gradually over the same time frame.

The miracle of the wine glass happened four months after my first visit to the delivery room as Carolyn's coach and months after I had completed a theology degree and was contemplating further study. The glass memorializes my prayers that day and God's reassurance that he loved me and knew my heart. I treasure it, remembering my awe at God's speaking so clearly to me. So much was happening—theological study, call to ministry, a new granddaughter, a house move, Stephen's health concerns, and issues at our church—it is not surprising that I did not act on God's visual reminder of his heart and his love for me.

In the past I had experienced periods of strong faith, weak faith, and almost no faith at all. I doubted, but I did not know I was being doubtful. When I ignored God's prompting through the Holy Spirit to be obedient to his will, he was still there. When I stopped reading the Bible and experienced the pleasures of the world, he used someone or something to give me reason to be obedient again. My life testifies to God's perfect patience. His patience can, however, come to its perfect limit. The Bible tells us that not everyone who says "Lord, Lord" will enter the kingdom of heaven, but only those whom Jesus has saved and who are obedient to God's laws and commands. Gradually I learned to trust and love the Bible, including God's laws, as David did, with my whole heart. His psalms helped soften my heart and long for God's Word.

I learned independence early in life. At nine I learned that life can be difficult, especially when the economy of a community halts abruptly. Our move to a new community was a complete reversal of lifestyle for me. As the oldest of six children I learned to take on adult responsibility because one of my siblings had special needs and my mother was expecting twins. Married at seventeen, and a mother at eighteen, I grew up quickly. My reality went from my parents' receiving their last baby bonus check (a Newfoundland parental benefit resulting from the 1949 confederation with Canada) for me in March to my receiving my first baby bonus check for my own son the following month, in April. Unrepented sin, heavy like the weight of shackles, holds us captive and distances us from a close relationship with God. Corb and I acknowledged the error of our ways, repented, and God lifted our burden of guilt, setting us free as the veil separating us from him was removed when he forgave us.

My faith in God grew because many of my personal needs were unmet by humans or institutions. I cried out to God in faith, because there was no one to help or comfort me. God's work in me, due to my reliance on him, is profoundly deep and mysterious. Unlike earthly loves and heroes, God never lets us down. When we trust God to grow our love for him and help us understand his Word and his ways, he is faithful to do so.

TRUSTING WITH A CIRCUMCISED HEART

I am grateful for the way that my grandmother, extended family members, and parents raised me. I did not need to champion women's movements. Many of my peers kept their maiden names, but I took Corb's surname. I also decided to attend his church. He was as strong a believer as I was, maybe stronger. We would have enough struggles as a couple without my adding the church that we attended to the list.

Throughout my life I felt misogyny at times, in both the

workplace and as a single mother. Due to my relying on the church to define Christianity and interpret the Bible, I saw God's Word as almost totally irrelevant, strongly patriarchal, and misogynistic. I adhered to the cultural, social church agenda for years until I read the Bible for myself. After studying it I saw my narrow-mindedness. There is nothing misogynist about God's Word, nor anything misogynist in Jesus or his ministry. Not only is all of the Bible relevant but the Old Testament shows that God loves women and men equally. By reconciling my ideas with a Christian worldview through the lens of the Bible, by early 2014 I realized that God's intent for my life was right, and best, and that he desires both men and women to trust, love, and serve him.

Israel valued literal circumcision as a covenantal promise between Hebrew men and God. Genesis 17 introduces this rite, but God reveals throughout the Bible that the circumcision of the heart is more than a sign of the flesh. It is invisible but equally painful. The Israelites' disobedience resulted in forty years of wandering in the wilderness because God had to humble them; they had to acknowledge that, although they were literally circumcised, their hearts were not and they were far from God.

Christians' circumcision, salvation or justification, too is unseen and spiritual. It is an inward sign of accepting Jesus Christ, God's fulfilment of covenant with us. On salvation, the Holy Spirit seals our hearts, that space reserved for God's infilling. God wants us to love and obey him, his laws, and his commandments. God wants hearts like his. We can only harden our own hearts against God so many times before he also hardens our hearts. God knows how easily we are duped into believing false doctrine and following false leaders who flatter us. Through the prophet Jeremiah God pleaded with his people to circumcise themselves and remove the foreskin of their hearts by submitting to his will (Jeremiah 4:4). God told them that they would find him when they sought him with their whole hearts (Jeremiah 29:13). A circumcised heart is a heart softened and submitted to God.

The covenant of circumcision indicated that the Israelites knew that God was the source of all truth and knowledge. The outward covenant of the inner promise God instituted with Abraham was a covenant of the flesh involving males that also had health benefits. Circumcision of the heart, however, applies equally to males and females. Although unseen and totally spiritual, its fruit is evident to God and to all believers. Circumcision opens the eyes of the heart, helping believers be less susceptible to sin.

No female can rely upon her relationship with her husband, father, or priest for her own salvation, just as no man can rely on his wife's or priest's. It was partly this realization of God's desire for each of us to come to him individually that spoke strongly to me of his call on my life. God had blessed me in so many ways. He had worked through everything that I had done, every mistake and every sin, to draw me closer to him. I knew that I must be totally obedient, trust him, and answer his call on my life, as he wanted me for a purpose.

Five generations, December 1998: Grandmother Vokey, Dad, me with Riley, and Derek

I may never have chosen to be a mother; I was, however, a mother at a young age. I did not want to be a teacher like my mother was. I wanted to do something and be someone more valued by society. That, however, was not God's intention, and being a teacher, a mother, and a grandmother was his working through my life. God knew my heart was not fully his. Although on salvation the Holy Spirit had circumcised my heart, intense spiritual transformation took, and is still taking, time, and for me came only through intensive biblical study.

A Child's Trusting Heart

God desires for us to have the trusting heart of a child. During thirty-two years of teaching and administering primary/elementary schools, I experienced moments of humility and openness with young children that is not usually present with older children and adults. I learned much about life, faith, and trust from them. Children generally are refreshingly honest and have few preconceived ideas or misconceptions. They are open, willing, and want to learn. Before they were adolescents, my children and my grandchildren believed what I taught them. Watching them grow has convicted me of the need for increased prayer for them.

In the summer of 2003, as Stephen was finishing his radiation treatments, we took my only grandson, Riley, on all-day outings with us. He would talk excitedly to us: "I have everything. I have my family, my sister, my mommy and my daddy." One day we were going to a beach some distance outside the city. A car struck us while we were stopped at a red light, and the three of us went by ambulance to the hospital, mainly because of Stephen's condition. At the hospital Riley thought he was in a mall, and he was curious about the black doctor caring for him, as he had not seen many, if any, black people before. Innocently, he wanted to know if the doctor was born that way. A bandage on his knee fixed everything, but Riley was concerned about Stephen, asking him, "Are you all right, Poppy?" Later on he asked Stephen if he would die before he grew up, which Stephen, despite his health condition and because of his faith, handled well, alleviating any fears Riley had. Young children are so delightful, but it does not take long before their childlike openness is marred by the world.

My memories of my grandchildren make me laugh and give me hope. During the advent of 2004 we were taking care of Riley, then six, and Marissa, age three. Riley was drawing pictures as gifts to place in the manger for Jesus. Marissa was also trying to draw pictures, but she was concerned that hers were not good enough, and people would not know what they were. Riley's person and tree looked like a person and a tree. She wanted him to draw pictures for her, and she whined a little. With patience and lovingkindness, Riley said to her, "You're doing a good job, Marissa. It doesn't matter what you draw because Jesus knows what you're thinking in your heart"—a theology lesson out of the mouth of a child.

My grandchildren know what gives me joy. They know how I value my "God books." They know that Christmas is the celebration of the birth of Jesus Christ and the main event regardless of the accuracy of his birth date. Likewise, when we celebrate Thanksgiving and the death and resurrection of Jesus, God is the focus, not the secular celebration. Maria, in 2012, then only four, made a three-dimensional Mary and Jesus scene that showed me that she understood how important Jesus's birth is to me.

GOD'S WILL, GOD'S WORD, GOD'S WAY

I appreciate the gifts of my parents, grandparents, and ancestors, as they contributed to my faith, but I am most grateful for my salvation and the circumcision of my heart. I thank God for the clear message of his Word. I trust in God with all of my heart and I do not lean on my own understanding. In all my ways I depend on him to lead me. These words from Proverbs 3:5–6 have been dear to my heart as I gradually allowed God through the Holy Spirit to build a visible, acting trust out of my once-small faith.

I am grateful for my children, my grandchildren, and God's working through their minds and hearts. I am blessed by God's refining me by, in, and through them. Most of all, I am grateful to be blessed by a steadfast, childlike trust in Jesus as Lord and Savior of my life as he shepherds me, mediates on my behalf to my Father, comforts and guides me through his Spirit, and nurtures me through his Word. I trust Jesus, the Holy Spirit, and the Bible to inform my thoughts, words, and deeds, and to lead me where the Father wants me to go.

CHAPTER 5

U: UNSEEN PRIORITY

By faith we understand that the universe was created
by the Word of God, so that what is seen was not
made out of things that are visible. (Hebrews 11:3)

*W*hat we believe about God and his Word matters. Where we
live or in which church we worship may have little significance for us
spiritually because Christ's church universal is invisible to all except
God, and only Jesus will determine who is in it. If we, through Jesus,
give God dominion over our lives and the Holy Spirit resides in us,
our priorities are spiritual. As the Holy Spirit breathes new life in us,
the unseen dimension is our priority.

FEAR OF THE UNSEEN

Children generally take things they cannot see or do not know on
faith, because they trust their parents. But all too soon they learn to
fear. Some adults, too, are afraid of what they cannot see or may not
understand. There have always been people who are afraid of what
they cannot explain but who are paradoxically fascinated and thrilled
by being afraid. Popular culture capitalizes on these fears. My sister
and I held blankets around our backs and our heads as we watched

TV shows about the supernatural—witches, ghosts, UFOs—that we perhaps should never have watched. Scaring people and being scared was the in-thing. This seems truer today, considering the popularity of the horror genre. Titillating, frightening myths and fantasies generate audiences and profits.

Ideas surrounding death have shifted from healthy respect and dignity to defiance and even ridicule in some circles. The pendulum swung from being uncomfortable talking about death to a morbid curiosity, filling lawns with tombstones and ghosts and even daring death to happen. Christian funerals and burials grounded in traditional church liturgy are no longer the norm. More and more television programs and Internet sites are dedicated to supernatural and paranormal activity. Christians know there is no good teaching around death, the spiritual, or the supernatural apart from the Bible. They trust in God and his Word to ensure protection against anything not of him.

Some parents attempt to shield their children from dimensions they say are superstitious, but young children gravitate easily to talking about spooky things, magic, and the unexplainable. If we watch children's programs on television or the Internet for a few minutes, this is confirmed. All too quickly children experience magic, illusion, and fantasy.

I believe that society's inability to reason and think critically is crippling our spirituality. We do children and society a disservice when we give them half-truths because we think they cannot grasp the entire truth. We should not stifle children's critical thinking but preview what they watch and equip them with the Word of God. Our society thrives on irrational fear but has lost its fear and awe for Almighty God. As Christians are denied opportunity to voice the truth, discuss how it is manipulated and withheld, it is not just the vulnerable who are exploited but all of society.

AN EMOTIONAL SIGN

I hesitated to share my glass story because it involved my emotions. It exposed my emotions and I was apprehensive that it might evoke emotional responses in others. I was heartbroken that day. I had difficulty accepting the glass as a sign, because I could not rationally explain it; I was uncertain of its origin and what it meant. Lately the verse "For the foolishness of God is wiser than men, and the weakness of God is stronger than men" (1 Corinthians 1:25) has made me wonder if I had been wallowing in the sins of pride and doubt.

After Stephen's death I shared my glass story with several believers, as the Holy Spirit convicted me of its significance. The way that Hannah desperately pleaded to God, speaking "in her heart, only her lips moved, and her voice was not heard" (1 Samuel 1:13), reflected how I felt. I do not know if my lips moved, but I was desperate about what was happening in my church in January 2008. I questioned whether my not sharing my story was disobedience.

God had answered my prayers before, but I had never received a visible sign. The glass sporting a beautiful heart was a physical object, but it reminded me of God's love and how he had sent Jesus, his only son, to save our broken world. The two pieces, fitting perfectly in the hole, reminded me of Jesus's body given for us, which is also broken, broken that we might be made perfectly whole through him. It reminded me that Jesus is the fulfilment of God's Word, and God's covenant with us links us to him as the two pieces fit perfectly together in the glass. God's heart must be constantly broken, as unrepentant hearts refuse to hear and obey his Word.

THE MEANING OF LIFE

Philosophy, psychology, and psychiatry, as interesting as they are to me, do not explain where I came from or why I am here. Much of the how and why of life, God, and creation remains a mystery. The Bible is sadly often omitted from discussions of the origin and purpose of life within much of the institutional church. Some believe we are eternal beings with a limited physical life on this earth; others, that this life is all there is. If we believe in a Creator God, then he alone authored everything, including science and philosophy. God is truth. When I realized in the late 1980s that I was God's child first, he overcame all my fear of heartache, adversity, and death, not just my childhood fears. I no longer feared what I did not understand; I knew that God was sovereign. God and his Word made me understand the true meaning of life. Through prayer and understanding the Bible, God helped me discern what was of him—what is most important.

THE SPIRITUAL DIMENSION

I discovered, as a young child, that God was real, more real than most of what I could see, feel, or hear. I was never alone. I was part of a much greater something that I could neither explain nor understand—from my first powerful connection with God as I prayed the Lord's Prayer and my prayer for action was answered affirmatively. Like any new Christian, saying yes to Jesus is just the beginning of a lifelong relationship requiring biblical faithfulness to know who God is.

In the past century, the West has embraced a pagan spirituality. Strange, eerie, tantalizing thrillers is good business, as there is much time—my grandparents called this idle time, but "idol" time is more accurate—to be entertained. As a young adult, I questioned and studied death, the supernatural, reincarnation, mediums, mystics, transcendental meditation, and Buddhism and other Eastern religions. I was fascinated by New Age writings that expounded on things that could not be seen and explained. I knew that life involved far more than I could see, especially after death, and I wanted answers about what comprised this unseen world. As a child of God, my understanding the spiritual dimension through God's Word brought repentance and further knowledge of spiritual things.

I was not totally convinced that there was an evil dimension until 1988 when I visited the Mayan ruins and pyramids. I will never forget the cold, heavy presence of evil. Later I learned that the area had been used for human sacrifice. The Bible taught me how shifty and conniving the devil is: he does not present himself as a black figure dressed in red with horns but as an angel of light. If we believe his lie that there is only the absence of good and there is no evil, we are hooked. Believers know that there is evil in the world and pray regularly for protection against the ruler of this world and his forces.

Many people rebel against the great and marvelous God of the Bible. In denying God, they have chosen to spend eternity without him. Parts of the institutional church have taught what is false or unnecessary to salvation while leaving out what is essential. The devil is the ultimate terrorist, playing havoc and using the church to build his empire, as many people still refuse to believe he exists.

I now know that what is most important in this life is what is unseen. Only God's Word reassures us what is of him and what is not. I no longer fear what I cannot see or fully understand; I am protected by my heavenly Father. There are two spiritual realms and two types of signs and wonders: good and evil. There have been many events in my life that I once put off as mere coincidence because to do otherwise seemed unsophisticated. Now I take the things of God as blessings and pray for protection against everything not of him.

SPIRITUAL EXPERIENCES, 1984

Corb was sick ten months before he died. We lived as normally as possible during those months, praying that God would heal him, but mine was a minimal faith. The summer of 1984 was spent in doctor's offices and at the hospital. Corb was sent home to die on his thirty-third birthday, but his needs were far too great for me to care for him at home. A kind and godly Christian doctor from another hospital agreed to try a round of experimental chemotherapy when our family doctor consulted him for assistance.

Corb had an uncontrollable nosebleed the night before he died. I was desperate because the doctor had told me earlier that week that the chemotherapy was not working and that the cancer was rapidly advancing. That night was the first time I earnestly prayed for God to take Corb quickly if it was not his will to heal him. It was the first time I relinquished my selfish desires to keep Corb alive. The next day, early Sunday afternoon, Corb died quickly and peacefully, literally in my arms, without anyone knowing he was so close to death, until the nurse checking on him could find no vital signs, and called for the doctor. Amazingly, Corb had a very short conversation with the doctor before rolling to his side. Then, with the doctor holding one hand and me cradling his head and holding his other hand, I told him I loved him and that I would care for our two children, as his spirit quietly left this world. For Corb this was a gentle relief from the pain and cares of this life; for me, the beginning of much pain, many cares, but also many blessings.

I knew God had heard my prayer. Did he answer in this way

because I had asked him to or was this just a coincidence? God was merciful and gracious to both of us by allowing Corb to slip so swiftly and peacefully into death without my fully understand what was happening. I was young, naive, and spiritually immature, yet I knew that Corb's spirit was no longer in the body on the bed. I was not completely sure where he was, but I knew that he was safe in the arms of Jesus because of his faith in God.

How many teenage boys would visit different local churches on Sunday mornings for worship? Corb and his friends did that when I met him. How many would talk seriously of faith as the most important thing in life with a family member just prior to his wedding? Corb did. I knew Corb's faith, not because we discussed it in depth but because he lived it.

After Corb's death I never felt alone. God's presence became more palpable especially as I read through the books of Psalms and Proverbs, and then on to the New Testament to find answers to my questions. I always felt God's loving and protective arms around me. Only once do I recall feeling unsafe, and that was at the Mayan ruins—but that was a spiritual not a physical threat.

I knew God was close, listening to me, answering prayer, and providing comfort and safety through the Holy Spirit as my faith grew stronger, even though I was angry with him for at least five years for not sparing Corb's life. There were too many spiritual, otherworldly experiences happening in my life for them to be merely coincidental.

Healing, Spring 2004

Our August 2003 car accident resulted in my having serious back and neck issues that persisted intermittently for almost a decade. For several years I went to physiotherapy and massage twice a week.

Because my back was weak and in constant spasm, my life revolved around the pain, what I could and could not do, including driving, because my movements were restricted, and still are. I could not bear to see cars in the rearview mirror. This apprehension, although not as bad, remains to this day.

The realization of the severity of my health issue came at Riley's bowling party that November when I dropped the first bowling ball I picked up. I could not lift it. At that moment my denial of my health issues evaporated. Nothing was alleviating my back problems, probably because I refused to take time off work. I loved my job; it was a crucial part of my identity. Frustration and irritation from the pain, discomfort, stiffness, and restricted movement in my back and neck were added to my list of complaints.

In spring 2004 a ministry team from Northern Ireland visited the church that Stephen and I attended. I went to the Holy Spirit workshop led by the Rev.'d Niall and Mrs. Geraldine Griffin of Colann Ministries, SOMA (Sharing of Ministries Abroad) Ireland. Not a firm believer in faith healing, and certainly never one to go forward for prayer, I was desperate enough to give it a try. After several minutes of being prayed over for my neck and back injury, I felt my spine move. As a skeptic and a control freak, it was an uncomfortable experience. I had attended several charismatic events before, but I usually left early because seeing people out of control or slain in the spirit unsettled me and I could not reconcile this phenomenon with anything I read in the Bible. The devil mimics anything which is of God, Jesus, or the Holy Spirit.

As I stood and Niall's hands were laid on my shoulders and several with him prayed over me for healing, my mid-spine section physically moved. Emotions stirred within me. My tears flowed for a long time. No one was more surprised by this than I was. Although I did not fall on the floor, I shook and trembled as I wept.

The closest I can come to describing the movement in my back was that it resembled the final wiggling sensation I felt both times I gave birth. After feeling the movement in my back, and the power of God's Spirit upon me, several that I laid my hands on and prayed over fell to the ground. A feeling of euphoria that I know to be the power of the Holy Spirit was around me. I had felt the power of the Holy Spirit before, but not like this. On Sunday morning I witnessed about my experience to my church congregation. This was the first time I had ever spoken in a church. It was out of character and outside my comfort zone, but I had to tell what God had done in me.

After that day I had partial physical healing in my back. I was not completely healed, but bones in my neck melded. I do not know how or why—the only thing I know absolutely is that my spine actually moved. I was powerfully touched physically, emotionally, and spiritually by something I cannot explain. During this time I also struggled with what I should do with the rest of my life. I did not want to leave the teaching profession, but I just could not bear the person I had become because of the chronic pain in my back and neck. With a heavy heart I retired and took a year to rest. During that time Stephen regularly encouraged me to do theology courses, which I fought long and hard.

THEOLOGICAL STUDY, 2005–2008

Stephen's persistence and my healing experience were the catalyst for my beginning theological studies in September 2005. My studies deepened my biblical knowledge and understanding as well as my relationship with God. Reading the Bible caused me to constantly search for more of God's truth, all the time asking for his help to understand it. More and more I depended on God and less on the world, as Jesus was also becoming Master and Lord of my life. The

New Testament, prayer, and the Holy Spirit became increasingly my sources of strength, but the Old Testament still made me uncomfortable.

While doing a course on the book of Revelation I wondered why Western theological thought varied so much from that of the third world, who held the Anglican church biblically accountable. To better understand this, I compared a Western and African exegesis of Revelation 12. God spoke to me clearly as I pored over the Bible. I could not understand how, or why, I had fought doing theological study when so much of civilization is founded on Christianity. When we picked up the bound copies of my thesis, Stephen said he felt as if we had given birth and, figuratively, we had, as he had proofread what I had written—and it had been hard work.

COINCIDENCES OR GOD SPEAKING?

Less than a year after my master's thesis was completed, in January 2008, I was in fervent prayer considering the state of the church and expressing my troubles to God when he provided the glass sign, about which I at first kept silent. After graduation I had focused on my family, especially after my granddaughter was born. I offered to care for her when my daughter returned to teaching. From September 2008 to June 2009 I rejoiced in my youngest grandchild, yet I strongly felt the call to ministry. In 2010, Lambert Publishing published my thesis. I knew that if Stephen and I were to later publish anything it would not be an academic book, but what and when God wanted.

My faith in God was much stronger when Stephen was diagnosed with cancer just after our fifth wedding anniversary in 2002 than it was in 1983/1984 when Corb was diagnosed, and died. My faith and Stephen's faith could withstand anything. Although the almost nine years of treatments allowed greater opportunity for us to get to know each other and God better, the last months were extremely difficult. Eight weeks in palliative care were taxing for Stephen, and I was close to exhaustion. Stephen and I knew that God would heal him or allow him to pass from this life in his time, not ours. God was in charge. Although he was in a palliative care unit, a place offering little or no hope of healing, we continued an alternative diet for as long as Stephen could tolerate it. We knew God was not going to call Stephen home until his purposes were fulfilled.

I prayed one Thursday evening that God would grant Stephen a peaceful end, if he was not going to heal him. This was the first time I had prayed in this way for him; all other prayers had been with confidence of healing. It was a similar prayer to the one I had prayed almost twenty-seven years earlier for Corb. Stephen's death came within three days of my prayer, quietly early in the morning on Thanksgiving Sunday. I did not realize that it was Thanksgiving weekend, because I was so wrapped up in Stephen's care that I had lost all sense of day and date. When I re-read my journals and reflect on that time, I know that Stephen suffered so much. I was exhausted from little sleep, and my left hand sprained from shifting him in the bed, as he could not move himself, and I too was ready to accept God's will. God's timing is always perfect. I gave thanks to Almighty God for His graceful and providential hand in allowing Stephen's death to unfold beautifully and peacefully.

On the morning of Stephen's death, I left the hospital quickly to tell his son, Richard, of his father's passing. Richard was still sleeping, as he had been with us late the night before. He was not surprised to hear the news. When I arrived home around 9:00 a.m., I called Stephen's mother and sister, both of whom lived in another province. After the funeral, Stephen's mother told me how she was asleep when I called. When the phone rang, she had been dreaming that she was rocking baby Stephen. Although she knew why I was calling, she felt completely peaceful, even though losing her son was difficult. Kim, Stephen's sister, shared how later the day that Stephen died, a green budgie with a yellow breast, just like his childhood budgie, perched on the railing of the back deck. For Kim, it was a sign that Stephen was fine.

I did not need a sign. I knew where Stephen was and I had no regrets, having loved him and done everything I could for him while he was alive. I was confident he was safe with Jesus. But God had a surprise for me. Stephen loved Pink Panther movies. A week before he died, he asked me to rent the new Pink Panther series. He tried to watch them from his hospital bed, but he could not stay awake. A few days before his death, he tried again, but he was so weak that, according to him, he could not get the nuances.

I knew Christmas 2011 would be difficult, but I was determined to celebrate Christ's birth with my family. A church close to our home presents a Christmas cantata early each December. Stephen and I could never go, as he was busy at his church and I was always busy at school. But we always talked about going. That year when I saw the sign advertising the Singing Christmas Tree, I was determined that this year I would go. I had no idea about the storyline, except that it would be a Christmas-themed performance involving a singing Christmas tree.

Riley, Marissa, Richard, and I went to the concert. It opened with a modern-day family discussing Christmas and its origin. About three songs into the performance, a detective came onstage to the unmistakable Pink Panther theme music. The four of us looked at each other, and smiled. What are the chances of Pink Panther theme music in a nativity musical? After the concert we talked about Stephen, each of us feeling true Christmas joy. We were all encouraged and comforted by this, knowing that Poppy Stephen was fine because he knew Jesus, and Jesus knew him. I was not looking for a sign, nor did I require one, but God gave us one.

Throughout the Bible we see how God has encouraged, comforted, and provided for his people in unconventional and unexpected ways. This Pink Panther story is just one humorous, yet significant, example of how God encouraged, comforted, and blessed me.

THE UNSEEN IS PRIORITY

God speaks to us through his Word. We often have difficulty understanding and discerning the unseen realms of God, but there is much in the Bible to comfort and guide us. Many men and women of God have spent their whole lives studying the Bible, because they obeyed his command to do so. Like them, and like Caleb and David before them, we too have the choice to read God's Word, and obey him.

God has protected, guided, and spoken to me in various ways throughout my life. While re-reading my journals, I realize there are many spiritual things that I cannot explain, much of which seemed unimportant at the time, but these unexplainable events have formed and strengthened my faith and trust in God to what it is today. Since January 2008, but especially since 2011, I have been more confident in praising and thanking God for his encouragement and reassurance through everything in my life, including the little miracles of every day. I have also been more consistent and diligent in praying for his protection against the devil. God commands us to use his Word to discern what is of him. At times God used Israel's enemies to achieve his purposes. I know God uses even my sin to my spiritual benefit.

Rainbows remind me of God's sure and certain love for me, despite my selfishness, pride, and sinfulness. Rainbows are also a reminder of God's covenant with Noah in Genesis 9, the pillar of cloud by day in Ezekiel 1, and of God's majesty as they encircle His throne in Revelation 4. All indicate God's love. I saw my first double rainbow while crossing the Sea of Galilee on my first trip to Israel, February 10, 2012. It was a dark, stormy day. Not everyone wanted to board the boat, but as the weather cleared, a beautiful double rainbow dispelled the dark clouds. It was a spectacular sight, especially as a scavenger flew in front of my camera. That rainbow is a special reminder of the spiritual space within us reserved solely for covenant with God. I thought how the Holy Spirit within me dispels darkness, bringing me light, just as the rainbow encircling the Galilee offered hope of sunshine.

Rainbow over the Sea of Galilee, February 10, 2012

Like Caleb and Joshua, as we begin to love God more, grow in fellowship with him, desire his truth above all, and seek him through his Word, with all of our hearts, minds, and souls, our spirits grow and we become more open to him. God helps us understand how his covenant is reflected in our hearts.

The more I study God's Word, the more I want to; the more I know about God's Word, the more I am blessed by what I cannot see. I cannot see the Holy Spirit, but I hear his voice; I cannot see God's hand, but I feel his touch; I cannot know God fully, but I am learning to understand some of his ways; I cannot know his every thought, but I am learning to know some of them. I cannot protect myself, but he protects me; I cannot know the way my life will unfold, but I am safe in his care as he leads and guides me. I am trusting more in what I cannot see and less in what I can as my unseen God is the priority of my life.

CHAPTER 6

M: MATTER IS SECONDARY

For I know that nothing good dwells in me, that is, in my flesh. For I have the desire to do what is right, but not the ability to carry it out. (Romans 7:18)

*B*efore the universe was made, God was. He always has been and always will be. We are exhorted to be in awe of him. He is the beginning of wisdom and insight. We are wise to be in awe of the power that created us and sustains us. Many people cling to the physical world that they can see and touch to the detriment of their spiritual well-being. Living for the world dulls our receptivity to God, who works through all things to reconcile us to himself.

LIAISON BETWEEN SPIRIT AND MATTER

If God, who is Spirit, is who he says he is, and if the Bible, passed down through thirty-four to forty faithful scribes over a span of one thousand to twelve hundred years, is God's Word, then I must follow it fully and faithfully. The Bible, God's inspired revelation of himself, written three thousand to nineteen hundred years ago helps us understand the vast chasm between us and God, just as Jesus, the Word made flesh, bridged the spirit-matter divide. The Dead Sea scrolls, found in Qumran between 1946 and 1956, written about one hundred and fifty years before Christ, confirm the accuracy of the Old Testament. Isaiah, the only complete book found, is almost identical to the book of Isaiah in today's Bibles, proving that the Old Testament changed little over two thousand years. These documents refute biblical criticism and liberal interpretation but support those who profess that the Bible is God's Word, the source of all truth.

Qumran, Israel, visited on February 15, 2012 and January 17, 2014

TEACHING AND LEARNING

Total honesty is what God commands—not withholding information or couching truth in gentler terms or euphemisms. Generally, people say they want the truth, but they are not truthful, maybe out of fear of reprisal or judgment. Honesty involves transparency, lovingly divulging information even when it is uncomfortable.

For Christians, God directs through the Bible that we should be honest even though we may not be well understood. Christians believe in a triune God they cannot see. They pray to God, through Jesus, who mediates on their behalf, and the Holy Spirit provides the strength they need to live as God commands. Although everything necessary for life is in the Bible, many who profess to be Christians do not use it as a guide. Increasingly these people rely on secondary sources as their base of truth. God alone knows how far we can step away from his Word and still be true to him. The Bible says there will come a day when there will be a great falling away and teachers will give their hearers what their itching ears want to hear.

If we think we have the power within us to do and be anything we desire, and we are the masters of our own destiny, then we deny God, becoming little gods ourselves. Some struggle to find meaning every day and wonder what they are missing; others for a time, decades even, live seemingly satisfying and fulfilling lives. One day many will have a rude awakening when life, as they know it, implodes.

Life can change drastically in the blink of an eye. Even though, as believers, we have the Holy Spirit indwelling us, there is an ongoing struggle between our physical bodies and what God commands us to do, between our spiritual nature and our own flesh, until we die. Then, equipped with the wisdom of God's Word, and through the power of the Holy Spirit, we can walk away from what is of the world and walk in faith with God.

Learning God's Will and Ways

After Solomon's downfall and Israel's subsequent division into two kingdoms, one especially wicked king of Israel, King Ahab, 873–852 BC, was brought to lower depths of depravity than Solomon when he married Jezebel of Sidon to seal a treaty with her father, the king of Phoenicia, a pagan high priest. Like her family, Jezebel worshipped Baal and used evil to get what she wanted. Ahab, who disobeyed God and his command not to marry outside of Israel, and Jezebel worshipped Baal. If the prophet Elijah had not overcome the prophets of Baal at Mount Carmel through his faith and God's raining down fire on these evil prophets, the world may have fallen into the hands of Baal, but God faithfully prevailed through Elijah. Near the end of his reign Ahab humbled himself and repented, but too much evil had been done. Due to Ahab's repentance, God withheld his judgment on his house until after his death, but prophecies surrounding his and Jezebel's deaths unfolded as foretold. Like them, we choose or reject faithfulness to God.

History attests to many unholy alliances. God speaks in his Word to all aspects of relationships, with whom to be associated and from whom to be set apart, but he gave marriage special attention. The marriage covenant impacts who the bride and groom will become both physically, socially, and spiritually, and, most important, future children of that liaison. The Bible tells how Ahab's and Jezebel's children were wicked and depraved. We may not be Ahabs and Jezebels, but, like them, we are selfish and we disobey God and his laws. We choose to listen to God through His Word or not. God clearly outlines who he is, his will, and his ways for us today as he did for those in biblical days.

The famous often go down the road of infamy. As years pass graves are rarely visited. Old graveyards grow over when no one comes to care for the plots, and sometimes they are moved, as the land they once occupied now serves a different purpose. Our souls and the Word of God, however, last forever. We grow closer to God when we suffer, and where the Bible is devalued or banned, its underground dissemination flourishes as believers hunger for the Word.

PHYSICAL EXISTENCE IS A GIFT FROM GOD

As a Christian who is being drawn closer to God each day, I look at life differently than a non-Christian, but life is a gift that I take for granted, and abuse. I thank God that he is gracious, mercifully kind, and patient with me. I marvel at how wonderfully we are made and how fine-tuned our earth is to meet our basic needs—the optimum temperature, oxygen, water, and food. I accept God, who created everything from our own planet earth, to the depths of the oceans, to far out into the stratosphere, to the farthest reaches of the cosmos, on faith. When I consider the vastness of the universe, it is easy to feel small, fragile, and insignificant. But when I am weak and vulnerable, I see the enormity of God's strength and love for me. I honor and appreciate all of God's gifts to me, but none compares to his first and most precious gift of life, which I am learning to treasure.

UNSEEN INTERSECTING MATTER

My broken glass, a tangible item, represents something otherworldly—one world intersecting another: the unseen in the seen. Why did this incident happen to me? Was I so weak and fragile that I needed a sign? Was I a likely candidate for the enemy? What kind of a vessel was I and what was the potter doing with me? God's speaking to me through the glass drove me further into his Word, making me reflect more deeply on it. Because the glass incident was such a personal, emotional experience, those biblical passages portraying emotions became more meaningful, especially David's psalms. Thinking of how the Holy Spirit guided Paul and the early church after Pentecost and guides us today I know that I should rejoice in God's provision.

God weaves everything together for his glory. He had and has a purpose for the glass—the creation of the heart in the physical object attests to an unseen force: energy colliding with matter. Does it have, and should it hold, meaning for others? I have prayed often about this. Some have said that if it is important to me, that is all that matters. But, is it? If it was a miraculous event, one that I should have proclaimed, but did not, then at the very least I should repent of my lack of faith. God speaks to us mainly through his Word and prayer, but sometimes he works through common tangible objects.

I hesitated to tell this story. By telling it, would I be building myself up? Who am I to be blessed by God in this way? Why would God let me know that he heard my heart? Why would he let me know that his heart was broken? Would it be any more or less prideful if I kept it to myself, because I was, in a sense, too proud to allow myself to be vulnerable and expose my life? I prayed that God would keep me from pride, and clarify his will. Either way would be challenging for me, perhaps telling the story more so, but I know it is his will, for whatever reason. I trust God completely. This entire story is God's story, not mine. It is a recounting of how God has impacted me.

I have pored over the Bible in the past five years trying to understand it, because it is his story—all sixty-six books together as one book reveal God—who he is and what he wants. Reading the Bible through quickly clarified God's metanarrative. Much happened in my life as a result of this glass. God has been my strength and sustenance for many years but he did not have my total loyalty until my heart was softened and quickened after Stephen's death.

I concluded that the glass incident could only be from God; he was encouraging me in my weakness. He wanted me to read and study his Word, so that I would share how he loves us. I felt that God wanted me to describe how he has transformed, and continues to transform, me, through his miraculous interventions, love, and mercy. I am learning to boast only in God—his love for me, his power, his strength, and his guidance in my life. I am learning to boast in knowing where to find the source of all truth and knowledge of him—in the Bible. I can feel God refashioning my heart into what he created it to be. It has not been easy but, as I become more his, and less entrenched in the world and its values, it gets easier. I do not worship the glass. It is an object representing the love of Almighty God.

God is Spirit, but he made matter and he made us. He sent his only son in physical form to bring us back to himself. For far too long I served my own agenda rather than obey God's laws, until God got my full attention. To a large extent believers have taken their focus off God and put it on that which they can see. God wants our hearts turned to him, not to the world. He desires that we allow him to circumcise our hearts so that the Holy Spirit may seal them for him.

THE CREATOR AND HIS CREATION

Loving and caring for God's world is what God desires; worshipping it is not. This is a line that is easily crossed. It is the small difference yet wide gulf of nurturing and tending our world versus worshipping it and placing it as priority, making creation a god. That is doing what God tells us not to do—nothing is to come between us and him. The sin of idolatry regularly caused the downfall of the Hebrew nation, and persists today. We are to worship God alone.

God has given us the responsibility of caring for his world. Caring for ourselves and for the universe, however, was not his first command—to love him with all of our hearts, souls, minds, and strength was. Then we are to love others as we love ourselves. If we replace love for God and others with a love of things, we sin against him. For years I grieved God as I valued material objects over him and people. I remember how, after Corb's death, I cherished things, because they did not die and, if lost, could be replaced. I have repented and been forgiven, but I still struggle with keeping this character flaw in check. Unfortunately, love of material possessions separates many from God and his love. We must thank God for, and rejoice in, the gifts he gives us, but we cannot allow ourselves to love the gifts above God. We can even, as believers, reach the point of eventually being thankful for our disabilities, adversities, and weaknesses, for these refine us.

MATTER AS PRIORITY

When people have no faith in God, it is easy for them to spend their lives focused on their physical existence and material possessions. Life seems attractive if it is accompanied by youth, strength, vibrancy, beauty, wealth, and popularity, but none of these last. The use of illegal and prescription drugs and alcohol is increasing, burying many victims prematurely. It is ironic that many who say that they love life the most spend vast amounts of money on substances trying to escape it. Those living solely for themselves are eventually faced with the fading of their health, beauty, and youth. In today's nihilistic society more and more young people are choosing suicide. There is also an increasingly popular right to choose death over life, even for the young and generally healthy.

Reality television is the latest addiction. The craze to become a star has impacted how we live: hairstyle, makeup, jewelry, and clothing are attention-getting tools in worship of the self. As Christians we know that the ruler of this world, Satan, has deceived and deceives many. Taking a stand for Jesus Christ not only takes courage but fortitude. Living a life for him should not be an educated versus uneducated debate, nor a self-sufficient versus needy debate; it is a conscientious choice one makes for the eternal good of one's soul.

We all think we know what it means to be wealthy. The poorest of the poor in the West are rich to many in other parts of the world and to the financially rich who are dying of incurable diseases. In the West many have an abundance of financial wealth. More and more are getting richer, while more are becoming poorer, financially. In the end not one person will take a single possession from this life. God does not want our money. He wants us. He wants our hearts. If we choose the world and idolize it to the detriment of our relationship with God and do not place him first as he commands us to do and as he deserves, we will pay a great price, far greater than all the wealth of the world.

PRIORITY MATTERS

God used circumcision and the sacrifice of animals as visual signs to teach Israel the importance of love, faithfulness, and obedience to him. God's covenant with Abraham and the ritual sacrifices ordained through Moses as he led his people out of Egypt were to teach them the importance of obedience. Obedience resulting in a circumcision of the heart was God's desired outcome. If believers do not obey God's commands, we will pay the ultimate price. Listening, heeding, and being obedient are generally not popular or well-developed skills in today's self-centered world; rather, being heard, adored, followed, and served is what is desired.

The prophet Samuel says that God delights in our obedience and listening to his voice. When David was anointed king, many expected him to be tall, but he was short. First Samuel chapter 16 describes how God revealed to Samuel the unimportance of height or physical appearance. Appearance is not a determiner of a person's faithfulness to God. God looks for persons whose obedience flows out of humble and faithful hearts. He is unconcerned about a person's looks, which fade through aging. Taking care of the body is not sinful, but how this is accomplished may be. God is interested in the heart; the world is interested in the physical body.

The Christian should not expect his or her struggles to follow God to be any different from those living in Abraham's, Moses's, or David's day. We must fear the Lord and serve him sincerely and faithfully. Human beings need God constantly. Life is difficult, stressful, all too brief, and joyless without him. If our day-to-day existence is our sole focus, we may have a pleasant life, but after a while it will become dull. If we choose our love of life over our love for God, we will suffer eternal consequences.

How are Christians to reconcile this conflict between what God commands and our desires? Only through salvation and growing closer to God through reading and meditating on his Word is it possible to please him and be with him in eternity. Christians believe in Christ's bodily resurrection and look forward to their subsequent heavenly bodies. We may live joyful and satisfying lives, but, in fact, we may be persecuted; we should be prepared for persecution, so that we do not waver under duress if and when it comes.

GOD FIRST

Believers will one day receive perfected bodies, but, until then, the heart is of the greatest importance to God. The circumcision of the flesh is the Old Covenant fulfilled through Jesus, the lamb slain as sacrifice for all time, satisfying God and covering our unrighteous, sinful nature. Through accepting Jesus, the ultimate sacrifice, we are redeemed and ready to be changed into who God wants us to be. The Bible emphasizes the importance of the condition of our hearts.

Faith in God is not commensurate with intelligence, wealth, success, skin color, or birthplace but on a personal relationship with God. He desires that we place our trust in him. He provided his Word for our edification, Son for our salvation, and Holy Spirit for our direction. Relationship with God is beyond the comprehension of many; to unbelievers, worshipping an invisible God does not make sense. Placing God first comes as the Holy Spirit and the Bible together illuminate our understanding and discernment as we grow spiritually into new creations. After a person is saved, his or her material and spiritual priorities change as the Holy Spirit begins the mighty work of sanctification of the heart.

Because God is sharpening my mind to understand how he works everything for my spiritual well-being, I seek him more each day. My first allegiance is to him. My next priority is studying the Bible and asking the Holy Spirit to help me to better understand it so that I may be a more faithful daughter and a better witness. With God as my Father and loving him before all others, the Bible as my guidebook, and the Holy Spirit to comfort and support me, I am well equipped to live the rest of my life abundantly in the love, hope, joy, and peace that much of the world does not understand.

CHAPTER 7

C: COURAGE IN CHRIST

The Lord is my light and my salvation; whom shall I
fear? The Lord is the stronghold of my life of whom
shall I be afraid? ... Wait for the Lord; be strong,
and let your heart take courage; wait for the Lord!
(Psalm 27:1, 14)

Although Christianity may be defined differently by many
religious traditions, belief in God and salvation through the blood
of Jesus Christ is the only requirement for a person to become a
Christian; this is authoritatively confirmed by God's Word. What
God has spoken through the Bible and what the Holy Spirit has
breathed into my spirit is largely contrary to the world in which I
live. Much of the world desires stability, prosperity, and peace for
themselves and their countries, but the God of Abraham, Isaac, and
Jacob, and the inspiration of the Bible, is not part of this equation.
Only God perfectly fills the aching, empty fissure of the heart
fashioned solely for him. I cannot imagine life without Jesus, and I
will not live my life apart from him; living in Jesus for God requires
supernatural courage that God alone provides through his Spirit.

COURAGE TO STAND

While my family environment nurtured faith in God, the culture I grew up in generally did not. Some people I knew went through the motions of being Christian but had double standards. When life is good, according to worldly standards, many people do not search for God. If we do not have a personal relationship with God, and follow manmade traditions, our thin veneer of "faith" erodes easily under the weight of trials and hardship. It is only my God-given courage of conviction in Christ that enables me to live for him: Christ lives within me (Galatians 2:20).

The early church knew how the sealing of the Holy Spirit and God's circumcision of the heart are tied to courage in Christ. Stephen, the first martyr, preached about a stiff-necked people uncircumcised in both heart and ears, resisting the Holy Spirit as their fathers had done (Acts 7:51). Both Jewish and Gentile believers showed tremendous courage in Christ once they were saved and filled with the Holy Spirit (Acts 10:44). From the time of the first church council in Jerusalem, around AD 48–49 (Acts 15), the disciples preached about God's searching the hearts of both Jews and Gentiles and cleansing them by faith. In Acts 16:14 we read of God's opening Lydia's heart. I believe this means that God circumcised her heart as she was converted to faith in Jesus. Courage to live in Christ and to stand in obedience to God's Word empowered by the Holy Spirit has been a necessary part of the church ever since.

IN THE WORLD, NOT OF IT

How many of us have gotten into the wrong car? Waited patiently at home all day for someone to make a delivery, only to find out they went to the wrong house—the house next door? Made a wrong turn at an intersection? Chosen the shortest queue, only to find that it took the longest time to get to the cash register? Sat in a pew at church and moved when someone told us that we were sitting in their pew? There are no wrong doors or pews with Jesus. He persistently knocks at the door of everyone's heart. He is the good shepherd eager to muster and lead the sheep, ever ready to bring people to God. Unlike sheep, we have the ability to open the door to allow him in.

How do we know when we make good or right choices? Augustine of Hippo said, "In essentials, unity; in non-essentials, liberty; and, in all things, charity." We must have the courage to stand by those essentials, which are necessary for salvation, and, at times, this takes much courage. Only God's Word describes the essentials of our faith. Freedom in non-essentials and love in all matters is easy when we are God's children united in Christ through the Bible. Then we can live peacefully in the world confident that we are of God, although the world may not wish to live peacefully with us.

COURAGE OF COMMITMENT

Once we believe on Christ for salvation, and desire to follow him, our lives often become more challenging. With Christ at the helm we have lives of peace, love, and joy surpassing all understanding, although we are in tension with the world's ways. Christians live for God and his purposes. Living for Christ in a Christ-less, selfish society takes courage, strength of character, and a strong identity as beloved children of God, qualities taught in God's Word. Seeking to be Jesus's followers as God expects is not easy, as we ache for those who seem oblivious to God, especially our loved ones. The dash between birth and death, what we do with those years, and why, is crucial. God created the world and it was good; humanity, very good. He wants us to enjoy our lives, lives that follow his created good order. God wants us to use the gifts he gave us: our abilities to reason, to have self-control, be morally strong, and to love others as he loves us.

Reflecting on what I enjoy—my family, music, art, and traveling—I see that everything is on a continuum between good and evil. If we consider music and contemplate how powerful lyrics are, we see how easily individuals are swayed by them. Some lyrics are dark and evil. The Holy Spirit helps us discern what is of God, including what we read or sing, but he does not do our work. We must listen to God in order to grow closer to him. As we do, we will not waver as we once did, because we are fully committed to Christ and his ways.

COURAGE TO UPHOLD THE TRUTH

It is up to us, both individually and corporately, as communities and nations, to choose to either learn from the mistakes of the past or not. The Israelites faithfully worshipped the one true God for a while, and then fell away to worship other gods and graven images. Then they returned to God, only to embrace pagan religion once again. We are no different. One generation faithfully serves God, the next falls away. Even in our own lives, there are months, even years, when we faithfully seek God, even serving him, followed by periods when we walk stubbornly on our own. Few Christians are faithful from the beginning of life to the end. This does not mean that we can deliberately take chances and live what we feel may be more enjoyable lives. Living for ourselves may jeopardize our relationship with Christ and, hence, our salvation.

In my younger, worldlier years, I cherry picked what I read of the Bible. I was a realist, generally uninterested in myths, especially those from what some felt to be an outdated, antiquated book, passed on by what was deemed a largely uneducated, unsophisticated, superstitious, fearful people. I had been religious, regularly attending church, but faith in God was not a way of life to be outwardly exhibited or shared. My belief system resembled an insurance policy rather than a manual for life. It is only now, after having studied God's Word, that I am developing the strength of character and courage of conviction worthy of a follower of Christ. I no longer follow people, but I am growing in courage to uphold God's truth.

COURAGE IN A DYING WORLD

We will all die. Believers know that they have the hope of eternal life even though this life may be fraught with hardships and abuse. David, despite his status and his grave sins, perhaps as a result of them, experienced heartache. With his heart turned to God, David pleaded for his grace, "Turn to me and be gracious to me, for I am lonely and afflicted" (Psalm 25:16). Such psalms pointed me to an all-sufficient, loving, steadfast, and long-suffering God. God's Word breathes life into broken and rejected people. Like balm for sore and bruised flesh it sustained me to face living in this world after Corb's death and after many other hurts and heartaches.

Being true to Jesus to the point of death is a lonely existence, from the world's standpoint. But when we say "Yes" to him, he will give us all that we need to be healthy in spirit, although physically and emotionally we may suffer. God equips and fortifies us for service. Being saved does not mean life will be easy or that we will never feel lonely or discouraged. While fear is not something a Christian should feel, periodic rimes of discouragement and weariness may be felt by some Christians in a world under siege by a foreign ruler. I have only ever borne up under the weight of oppression through God's strength, but it has been tiring and discouraging at times.

Like the Israelites under Egyptian domination by pharaohs, we live in a world where evil reigns and living for Christ is a constant battle. At times life is unfair, cruel, and unbearable. There may be days when we feel it is only us and God. We can be discouraged when we feel we are facing a giant wave on an uphill climb and we see few rocks for shelter, but God is always there just as he was for his chosen people. Jews and Christians alike love the story of David and Goliath. David's reliance on God gave him courage and saved him, not his own strength. God knew David's heart and used him mightily for his purposes.

We too are to stand firm and steadfast in our faith, with patient endurance. We must be courageous in the face of adversity: God is with us and will provide our every need. No Christian is spiritually healthy without God's complete covering. Eliminating sinful activities and disciplining myself to regular prayer and meaningful Bible study necessitates self-denial. God supports me most when I am at my weakest. I have seen the strength of God with those mourning, those fighting terrible addictions, and at the bedside of dying loved ones suffering while eagerly waiting to embrace Jesus. Many dear people quote the Bible, sing hymns and choruses, and are brave, fearsome prayer warriors, or quiet, gentle pillars of faith as they await their physical deaths and eternal life.

Some Bible stories resonated more with me as a child than others, and still do. Two—the story of the fiery furnace and the lions' den—involved the faithful Hebrew Daniel. During the Babylonian exile in the sixth century BC, Daniel, under kings Nebuchadnezzar, Belshazzar, Darius, and Cyrus of Persia, stood strong and firm in his faith, and influenced Shadrach, Meshach, and Abednego to do the same. With their youth, good looks, intelligence, and strong work ethic, the four friends were respected by the court in which they served. They are exemplars of courage for us today.

> Shadrach, Meshach and Abednego answered and said to the king, "O Nebuchadnezzar, we have no need to answer you in this matter. If this be so, our God whom we serve is able to deliver us from the burning fiery furnace, and He will deliver us out of your hand, O king. But if not, be it known to you, O king, that we will not serve your gods or worship the golden image that you have set up." (Daniel 3:16–18)

Daniel and his friends did not object to assimilation in the Babylonian culture that changed their Hebrew names to names derived from their idols or attending Babylonian schools. It was the corrupting of their bodies, the temples of God, by consuming the king's food and drinking wine with him at his table, where Daniel and his friends drew the line. Without the support of family or other God-fearing Hebrews, they stood their ground to the threat of death. Nothing came between them and God. Nothing should come between us and God.

Daniel studied and obeyed the Mosaic law, loved God and his Word, and was totally committed to it; God protected him and gave him prophetic words. As he stood firm in his conviction to God, Daniel was a godly example to his friends, the kings, and those all around him. He knew that God would hear his prayers, and so his thoughts did not waver. Because Daniel walked with, showed obedience to, and stayed true to God, he and his friends were miraculously spared. Daniel held on to his faith in God regardless of the consequences. He knew others were killed because of their disobedience to the king, but he refused to compromise. He would not bow down to another god, no matter the cost: Daniel worshipped the one and only true God. He is a godly example for us to be fearlessly courageous for Christ today.

How would we rate, in terms of unwavering courage, in the face of execution for our beliefs, in comparison to Daniel and his three friends? Are we immovable in our conviction of God's moral truths or do we compromise and believe there is no absolute moral truth anyway? Would we die for our faith? We experience tension, not balance or compromise, with the world, when we stand firm with God and his ways, as recorded in the Bible, rather than capitulate to the world's ways and demands.

GOD'S ENCOURAGEMENT

If Jesus needed God's encouragement, how much more we need it! God has provided encouragement when I have needed it most. He knows far better than I could ever know exactly what I need and when I need it to be buoyed up to serve him. The glass was a sign of encouragement, telling me that God is not an absent watchmaker, as he is presented by some theologians. It was and is a symbol of his love for me, a call to grow closer to him by studying his Word more deeply, especially the Old Testament, and to welcome his purposes for my life. Although I may not always sense his presence, I have learned to trust him completely. I must keep praying for, and entrusting completely to him, all those whom I love. This has been challenging, as I have always wanted to be in control, but, with God's help, I am learning to let go what he wants me to let go. I entrust my loved ones to him, knowing that they have the free will to accept his offer or not. The best I can do for those I love is to love them and pray for them.

COURAGE TO LIVE FOR GOD

Corb's diagnosis of non-Hodgkin's lymphoma and his death, just ten months later, completely devastated me. The love of my life had left me to raise our two children alone. My eyes were so sore from crying the first week after his death that the skin on my lower lids was raw. My stubbornness kept me from relying on over-the-counter or prescription medication to ease my pain. I also did not resort to alcohol or drugs, but I do not think many would have condemned me if I had, for too many in our culture rely on these routinely to cope with life.

No one, however, recommended counseling. It would not have made much sense to me, having graduated with an education degree, with a major in psychology. I remember thinking, *How could anyone, no matter their educational qualifications, give advice to me, if they had not experienced similar loss themselves?* At my time of deepest grief, I sensed that even some church leaders were uncomfortable with death. Over the years my limited experiences with illness, death, and dying deepened my faith and trust in God's loving power. I realized that there is no closer intimacy than being with loved ones as they leave this world, especially with those dying in Christ.

Following the deaths of my two husbands, when some well-meaning Christians called or visited me some of their comments were unsettling, as they indicated little or no faith. I wept for them, not for me or for those who had died. Learning that death is the beginning of eternal life with Jesus removes all fear of dying. When we submit to God's ways, allowing him to circumcise our hearts, we realize that there is someone who knows everything far better than we do and he provides the courage needed to lean on, rest in, and live for him. Because we know God through Christ, and know our destination upon death, we are fully free to live in the here and now for God.

NEW GROWTH AFTER THE FIRE

After Corb died, I do not know how or why I came to read the psalms. It may have been the comfort I found in Psalm 23 or my love for poetry that led me there. I sought meaning and purpose in life through various speakers and seminars, psychological and motivational literature, but none of these answered my questions. The psalms, however, were indescribably comforting. Through them God provided the courage and encouragement I needed to go on.

God is the master artisan, the master potter. I have felt, in some ways, like I have been through a kiln several times. On my last visit to Israel in September-October 2015, our Shiloh guide remarked on the vast numbers of potsherds all over the country, and how that, when these pieces are reused in new pots, the reworked pieces are even stronger than the original ones. This is a good analogy of how God reworks us broken vessels, making us much stronger each time. With every physical, emotional, spiritual, and familial loss and every challenge I faced, God reworked me, making me emotionally, mentally, and spiritually stronger.

And so I tasted and tested Psalms, Proverbs, and the New Testament, and I learned that God is good, although he allows bad things to happen to good people. There are far worse things than death. Corb was with Jesus. I was going to be fine, because God knew me and he loved me, and he is not restricted by time, space, or finances. My all-wise God comforted and faithfully provided much-needed rest for my weary soul. I knew he blesses all who mourn, and that included me.

After coming out of grief's fire, there was a time of refreshment, followed by new growth, like the fresh and tender regrowth of a charred area after a forest fire. This regrowth is not easily explained, but I have been its beneficiary. I thank God for his awesome love, mercy, patience, and provision during those years. As I read the New Testament, he comforted me, breathing into me deeper understanding and courage. Due to my loving but strict father I found it easy to relate with God as Father and my source of courage, strength, and love. As I became a more obedient child, I learned to take care in my conduct, as he who called me is holy and he calls me to be holy. I struggled with the concept of a call to holiness because I knew it could lead to legalism and fundamentalism, but God honors our prayer and study and breathes clarity into us.

I lived in a world of career, family, and single parenting. I supported my church by my attendance and financial gifts. I was fed spiritually by Bible readings and the lyrics of what I sang in church. The liberality sometimes espoused in the pulpit did not impact my soul like the soothing lines of God's Word that I sang did. I was blind, but now I see. My mind had to be opened and my heart softened to read a book that was publicly dismissed and ridiculed.

Reading the Bible and seeing how God's time is not ours has encouraged me to wait patiently upon him. The psalms of David are wise and comforting to me because he *knew* God, and I could see how his heart was wrenched because of his pain. In 1 Chronicles 28 David charged his son, Solomon, to know God and serve him with a whole heart and willing mind, because God searches all hearts. David admonished Solomon to be strong, courageous, and unafraid, because God is always with him, and in Psalm 31:24 he exhorts all who wait for him to be strong and let their hearts take courage.

As a young widow, I remember thinking, *A wealthy man would gladly give up his wealth for health, but a wise, healthy man would never give up his health for wealth.* That surely, also, meant spiritual health. My priorities for my own life and happiness and for that of my children began to change as my faith and trust in God grew. I was no longer impressed by the rich and famous; I found their selfishness, excessive materialism, and wanton, sinful existences pitifully sad. It was as if I was beginning to see with new eyes. God was giving me courage and changing my heart.

Statue of David, Citadel of David, Jerusalem, February 2012

At times I found life to be more complex and uncanny than fiction. As a single working mother, raising two children was only possible as God strengthened me with his love as I read his Word. I found myself becoming bolder in what I proclaimed about God, because I felt closer to him and more distant from worldly excesses and falsehoods. God helped me understand what really mattered. I knew that unless God ordained anything in my life, it would not occur. He knew when my heart was less than sincere. He gave me the courage to repent, change, and be within his will.

TAKE COURAGE COURAGEOUSLY

One of my favorite stories from the Old Testament is found in Joshua 1. It became even more so after my two granddaughters attended a "Kingdom Rock" Vacation Bible School (copyright 2013), and sang the songs from the Kingdom Rock DVDs, which they loved. "Stand Together" begins, "We will trust, trust in God alone; / We will stand, stand upon his Word, / And whatever comes our way, / We are strong, and we are brave." This catchy song reminded me of the Joshua passage that I was studying, and I found myself regularly singing it.

I have always been puzzled why Moses, who led the Israelites when the Lord redeemed them from bondage in Egypt, and formalized God's covenantal love for them at Mount Sinai, was not permitted to go into the Promised Land. After studying about Moses, Joshua, and Caleb, and reflecting on the pertinent biblical passages, I understood fully that God sees and knows those parts of us that we cannot see ourselves.

> Only be strong and very courageous, being careful
> to do according to all the law that Moses my servant
> commanded you. Do not turn from it to the right
> hand or to the left, that you may have good success
> wherever you go. This Book of the Law shall not
> depart from your mouth, but you shall meditate on
> it day and night, so that you may be careful to do
> according to all that is written in it. For that you
> will make your way prosperous, and then you will
> have good success. Have I not commanded you? Be
> strong and courageous. Do not be frightened and
> do not be dismayed, for the Lord your God is with
> you wherever you go. (Joshua 1:7–9)

The Israelites were upset because Moses would not be leading them into the Promised Land. God encouraged Joshua by telling him repeatedly that he was with him. Joshua had to be obedient to the laws Moses had taught him before he could be successful. Through his being strong and courageous, Joshua would lead Israel to inherit their land and be only one of two in his generation to see it. I identified with this passage in Joshua 1 because I hoped Stephen and I would work together in ministry, that he would lead the way, but this was not God's will. Now I minister without him, in whatever ways God leads and directs me. I study and store up God's Word in my heart so that I might sin less against him and be of good courage.

Some do not like Moses's story, as they think God was unfair. But God *is* God, the only one who is perfectly just. I strived after perfection for years but could never achieve it. Far worse than not having our dreams fulfilled is eternal separation from God. We desperately need God's help to change things in our lives that displease him so that we may serve him. With faith in Jesus comes commitment to him that further emboldens and empowers us to reach out to others and to live a life worthy of him. As we walk with greater courage and commitment, we more clearly understand what God expects of us as the Holy Spirit provides the courage necessary to stand firmly and boldly on God's Word.

COURAGE TO PROCLAIM

As a child I prayed to God through Jesus, but I at times wondered how this could have been at such a young age. I committed myself to the Lord, I trusted in him with a childlike faith, and God heard my prayers. With a grandmother who loved Jesus, and attending a church where the Bible was read, believed, and taught, and where Christmas was, first of all, the birth of Christ, through a virgin, and where Jesus rose bodily from the grave. I was given the greatest gift of all—a sure, solid, and firm foundation of belief in God. My understanding of the Holy Spirit, however, took years to fine-tune. Such concepts and relationships are difficult to verbalize, especially for young children, but not to live out.

I had little difficulty understanding that Jesus is the only perfect human being and that he is also God. At home, church, and school, we were grounded in Jesus's teachings, the Ten Commandments, and the golden rule. It was a rich environment to be raised in, and it provided a good moral base for knowing and loving God. But believing that the entire Bible is absolute truth came much later in my life. My lack of biblical literacy and my secular university education did not hamper my enthusiasm to learn more about God; he drew me closer through adversity. My quest to know drove my desire to learn more about God and his Word after Stephen's death, because of Stephen's persistence to do theological studies, and through the power of the Holy Spirit.

CLARITY AND CONFIDENCE

Jesus does not need part-time followers—there are plenty already. He does not want someone willing to work weekends or who are concerned about working conditions and benefits. When you understand, know, love Jesus, and have the power of the Holy Spirit indwelling you and realize that you cannot keep him to yourself, it is a full-time commitment. It is, however, not easy to stand courageously in the world with Jesus and his teachings. It is not for the faint of heart. It is for the bold and courageous, like Joshua, Daniel, Jesus, the apostles, the disciples, all the martyrs that ever died, and those dying for Christ today. Anything less is of the world, and we know what the Bible tells us about that.

Our life is a paradox. It seems all too brief, yet containing what seems like several lifetimes of memories. I look on my life as a flash book I had as a child. While thumbing rapidly through the pages you saw that it told a story. We are to treasure each moment as a gift from God; he has purpose for every second of every day, and much greater clarity comes when you know you are his. The light of the gospel dispels darkness, doubt, fear, and confusion. As I mature in Christ, I understand God more clearly each day. With clarity comes the confidence to live as God commands and to proclaim his life-giving message of salvation and hope through Jesus Christ.

To be fully committed to Jesus involves loving all that he loved, including the Old Testament. He knew the commandments and the laws far better than the scribes and Pharisees of his day. Knowing and loving the Old Testament have made my life sweeter, and it is easier to comply with God's wishes because I have a deeper understanding of Christ in his full humanity.

COURAGE FOR THE JOURNEY

I know how easy it is to sin and how difficult it is to repent and seek forgiveness. I know how easy it is to fool myself into thinking that my heart is right with God when it might not be, although my heart has been circumcised. Only God understands my heart. If Abraham, Moses, David, Solomon, Paul, and all of God's faithful ones could so easily miss the mark, I can too. I need God's protection to guard my heart against anything that is not of him, and the Holy Spirit's guidance to keep me to the narrow gate. I need God's Word to give me the courage to face the truth about myself. This can only be done by listening to God's voice through the Holy Spirit in prayer and meditation on what his Word says, not what I think or hope it says.

Jesus is the only source of living water to cleanse and refresh. He is faithful to nurture all who call on his name. He assures me that he is with me. He tells me to not be dismayed, for he is my God. I am confident that he will continue to strengthen me, help me, and uphold me with his omnipotent hand regardless of what life brings. Life today is especially tense for Christ's flock, but God equips us to faithfully follow the narrow path to victory in Jesus. From the overabundance of God's love to all who honestly seek him and the truth of his Word flow rivers of life, giving us courage so that we, in turn, may bless and encourage others to follow him.

CHAPTER 8

I: INTENTIONAL INTIMACY

The aim of our charge is love that issues from a
pure heart and a good conscience and a sincere
faith. (1 Timothy 1:5)

$\mathcal{S}$aved by grace, with our identity secure as God's children, we are
called into personal intimacy with God through Christ in the power
of the Holy Spirit. Commitment to God brings a greater desire and
responsibility to love him, and to love others as he loves them. Paul's
charge to Timothy to love from a pure heart, with a good conscience
and sincere faith, is only possible with a heart that has submitted
to God's process of transformation. A circumcised heart is turned
to God through Christ and is willingly being conformed into the
person he calls us to be.

WHAT IS LOVE?

"All you need is love," "Love makes the world go round," "With love
all things are possible"—in popular slogans the word *love* is bandied
about as if it were the cure for all ills, and Christians know, in at
least one way, this is true. Jesus came to earth from heaven to save us
from our sin and depravity. His is genuine love, not to be confused

with the disposable, user-beware, cookie-cutter love common today. Much of our world has difficulty recognizing true love because it does not know God.

One popular Bible passage about love comes from 1 Corinthians 13, often read at weddings. It espouses the value of love, then places it on a pedestal as the most important virtue of all. Verse 4 begins, "Love is patient and kind; love does not envy or boast; it is not arrogant or rude. It does not insist on its own way; it is not irritable or resentful; it does not rejoice at wrongdoing, but rejoices with the truth. Love bears all things, believes all things, hopes all things, and endures all things." Verse 8 begins, "Love never ends." A world that does not believe in absolute truth but insists on its own truth and rejoices in defining, making, and terminating love whenever, wherever, however, and, as often as it pleases, would be hypocritical in defiling such a beautiful passage. All too often, it does just that. Mixing God's ways with the world's ways cannot and does not work.

The world's definition of love is considered to be whatever is perceived as enjoyable, pleasurable, and far less demanding or judgmental than the love of God. This may be so if your lifestyle, or that of someone you love or respect, is in conflict with what God's Word teaches. Christians, on the other hand, are to mirror the love of God to each other and to the world. Those who know and love God and are growing in intimacy with him more each day experience tension with the world. Christians, though, neither hate nor participate in violence: both are contrary to God's commands. The world demands compromise and tolerance. It does not like tension but it is impossible for believers to live an authentic life for Jesus and follow God's direction to love as he does without tension with those who love the world.

GOD'S LOVE

The world often wrongly equates lust and sexuality with love, but the words used for love never equate with these things in the Bible. Love may be romantic, familial, and brotherly, but God's love is more than any of these. God's love is perfectly selfless, forgiving, and sacrificial.

As a young child growing up in comparative affluence, I was precocious, manipulative, and selfish. I thought that if my parents really loved me they would let me do and have what I wanted. This is how many children think, and they try to push the boundaries. Most parents learn that love is not always giving their children what they want, just as God does not always give us what we want. True love sometimes means saying no. I found it was sometimes easier, but not always best, for me to say yes to my children. If I, in my human weakness, can know what is good for my own children, how great are all those things that God desires for us.

I sought God to get what I wanted: his healing, his comfort, his listening ear. I viewed him as a big daddy in the sky. I understand now why God did not always give me affirmative responses. With a greater faith, trust, and biblical maturity, I see now that God does not grant my every request, especially if I approach him to achieve something I desire, yet my heart is far from him.

This made sense as I read about the Israelites using the Ark of the Covenant as a charm. They brought it into war for victory, in 1 Samuel 4, but victory was not theirs, and they suffered for their selfish intentions. Through a better understanding of the Old Testament I now liken my early prayers and petitions to the Israelites' use of the Ark. God requires that we approach him with a genuine, honest, loving heart before we can have a personal relationship with him. He wants us to know him, through his Word, sincere prayer, and listening to the Holy Spirit. God desires deep intentional intimacy—with our hearts and minds totally focused on him, to know and love him for who he is—not rote and mindless repetition of words that hold little meaning, as our hearts and minds are far from him.

Love Says I Am Sorry

Unlike the song from a famous motion picture that says "Love is never having to say you're sorry," apologizing and being forgiven are key to true intimacy with God. Our faith in him is based on Christ's sacrifice on the cross, our acceptance of his sacrifice, and our repentance and turning from sin. A circumcised heart has turned from sin in repentance and seeks forgiveness for sinning. God forgives when we ask for his forgiveness. We are wise, however, to remember what we have done that is sinful and hurtful to God so that we do not become repeat offenders.

The closer he draws us, the more we draw close to him; the more we love him, the easier it is to resist temptation. Our honest efforts please God. We must not fall into the sin of pride, thinking that we did something good in our own strength. We can only repent through Jesus's blood, with the indwelling Holy Spirit convicting us of our sin and making us want to change. A circumcised heart wants to say it is sorry for every hurt because it has been reborn, fashioned by God's perfectly loving and tender heart.

God's Perfect Intimacy

The analogy of Christ and the church to husband and wife is God's perfect example of intimacy. God is also described as the husband of

Israel in the Old Testament. A metaphor of the marriage covenant runs through the Bible. We usually think of Jesus as the bridegroom coming for his church, his bride, as solely a Christian belief, but it is also part of Judaism.

The Bible tells us that as the head of the home a husband is to love his wife as Christ loved the church and gave himself for her. That is an extremely high expectation. We, in selfish and imperfect physical bodies, cannot understand God's perfect love for us, but he helps us to understand when we read his Word. Nothing can compare to a strong knowledge of his entire love story to help us understand his persistent, patient, steadfast, sustaining, and life-giving love for us. God has been lovingly patient with me, even though I was willfully stubborn. Thankfully he loves us beyond measure. When I think of the love that welled up inside me after the birth of my two children when I first saw them, and later my two granddaughters, and the first time I saw my other grandchildren, I know I cannot begin to fathom the awesome love of God.

It is impossible while in the flesh to experience the fullness of God's perfect love for us because we could not tolerate it. We were made to be loved by God, to love him, and to love others as he loves us. We may feel that loving God is easy if we believe in him, but when our love is tested, and things do not go our way, we see that it is not easily achieved if our hearts are far from him. Loving all that God is and desires, and putting his will ahead of our own, is difficult. To love as Christ did, by laying his life down sacrificially, is the ultimate love. Christ's love for us is far more than a bridegroom's love for his wife. Despite the enormity of his sacrifice and his perfect love, truth, and generosity, he was rejected by those he came to save. He is still rejected today.

LOVING AS GOD LOVES

The word *unconditional* is used often in terms of love. Many claim they just want to be loved unconditionally. When Jesus struggled with Satan and with his impending crucifixion, he loved God unconditionally, as his perfect love for God cast out all fear and he overcame all temptation.

Although the Bible supports God's loving us unconditionally, because we cannot do anything to deserve his love, his loving us does not mean that one day we may not be separated from him. Once we choose God through Christ, we say yes to a new heart and we live for him every minute of every day. God will never lose his love for us, but we may choose to reject him, thereby being rejected by him. As God's children we are to be set apart as his light for the world. We are to act on his behalf. God's will and his way are perfect. We choose it or we do not.

To try to love as God does and to stand for what he stands for takes courage and strength of character that only he can provide. We must be intimate enough with God to be able to ask him to help us understand what we need and to provide it so that we can do all he asks us to do. Ultimately we are called to love the unlovable unconditionally, as he does. We are to pray for and love everyone, especially our enemies. We are to know and speak God's whole truth courageously in love, not just the parts that we like. Teaching the truth of the Bible in love does not mean that we are to judge anyone. God's Word is like a two-edged sword, separating his absolute truth from what is not. Only Jesus will judge, and we leave that to him. We are constantly being purified by our obedience to God. However, as much as we study God's Word, obey, and love him, we will only love him with our imperfect human ability to love.

A WOMAN'S LOVE

....

I was privileged to grow to age ten feeling safe and cherished. I remember crying myself to sleep, afraid that something might happen to Grandmother Vokey. Although I know my parents loved me, the bond between my grandmother and me was special, and her relationship with God so evident in her life that her relationship with me was pivotal to my spiritual formation. I was extremely close to her in childhood but we were separated geographically just before I married.

When I reflect on God's creation of a perfect universe, the first couple in the garden falling through disobedience, and how the woman enticed by the serpent subsequently enticed her husband, her punishment in childbirth makes sense to me. Childbirth is painful. With my first child, I was in labor over twenty hours before going to the hospital, before telling anyone, because Corb was at work. Prolonging the visit to the hospital made childbirth and delivery more bearable. My second delivery, however, was more difficult; I was hospitalized for a week, waiting to be induced. Through childbirth, I learned what God meant by having difficulty in childbirth. Giving birth is hard, painful work, but both times I knew that God was with me in my agony. The joy in giving birth, or of being present as coach, and holding children or grandchildren, however, far outweighs any amount of pain experienced in childbirth.

The greatest part of my struggle to God's call on my life to ordained ministry was associated with my gender. About twenty-five years ago I studied the Bible's position on women in ministry, as it was an issue in a local church. My conclusion: Jesus would have agreed to the ordination of some women, just as he would agree for some men who feel called. However, I struggled with my own ordination. Maybe I saw that if I was prevented from being ordained because of my gender that would provide a selfish way out for me; I had retired from a teaching career and I was ready to travel and spend quality time, months at a time, resting somewhere in the sun or traveling the world. I did not want another full-time job, not even one that paid.

God has a way of getting our attention, though. Amidst Stephen's illness, a life-changing car accident, theological studies, thesis study and writing, small miracles, babies being born that we thought might never be born, moving houses, alternative treatments to find a cancer cure, Stephen's death, an African women's Bible study group, and an Old Testament study, God made it clear that ordained ministry was his will for my life. The question I had to answer was, did I love God and his will more than I loved my life and my will?

A pivotal point in my call to ministry came around 2010 as a result of volunteering in a men's prison. If I had listened to Stephen and acted on my initial feelings, I would not have returned to the prison the second week, as my first visit was intimidating and out of my comfort zone. God used my persistence in never giving up on anything to return the next week. During the second week one man identified me as his former school principal. His sharing made me realize how many children fall through the cracks of our school systems, and it made me want to help those who did not have the supports I had had as a child. Most of them did not know God through Jesus, either. Teaching about the Bible was especially relevant with offenders. Most were, and are, eager to learn. Some, I discovered, I had taught or known years ago in the school system. God clearly directed me throughout the whole process.

I had difficulty reconciling 1 Timothy 2:12, the one passage in which Paul does not permit women to teach or to exercise authority over a man; as I resolved Paul's concerns in light of the Bible and God's call on my life, my apprehension about that passage disappeared.

God works through female servants and witnesses today as he has always done. Churches that promulgate misogynist teachings and biblical heresy will be held accountable. Many women in the Bible served God: Hannah, Ruth, Naomi, Esther, Mary Magdalene, and Phoebe, to name a few. The woman at the well, the first evangelist, brought men and women back to the well to meet Jesus. What is needed are honest people dedicated to God's call, regardless of gender, people saved by grace, who love and are well grounded in God's Word and will work passionately to serve and please him.

Serving God has little to do with the body and everything to do with the condition of the heart. Circumcision of the flesh, as God commanded Abraham, was the beginning. God desires heart circumcision. God tests each heart just as he tested the hearts of all the kings, especially King Hezekiah; he also tested Hannah, Mary, and Elizabeth. God tests my heart. He upheld me throughout the call, discernment, and ordination. He strengthens me constantly. What can mortal man do to me? I fear God alone.

THE WORLD DOES NOT LOVE US

The peace of God, which passes all understanding, guards my heart and soul so that God's truth—that which is honorable, just, and pure—is what I think about. There is much in life that is good, to be in awe of, and thankful for, in God's creation, yet so much to be wary of.

In the West we can still read the Bible, talk about it, and study it, without fear of retribution, imprisonment, or worse. This may not be the case much longer. We are cautioned in Matthew to know the signs of the age; the signs seem to say that the second coming of Jesus is near, although we are not to know the precise day, hour, or year. As his return approaches, the pressure on Christians to conform to the thinking of secular society will increase. Already in the West many Christians have denied the inspiration, inerrancy, and authority of the Bible.

Christians are being persecuted and killed every day for their faith. In some countries belief alone is a death sentence; other believers are imprisoned for carrying a Bible or for sharing the good news of the gospel. Even though we Christians are compassionate and kind, the world is offended by us when we oppose its values, those which are contrary to God's laws. Many have hard hearts, seared consciences, closed eyes, and shut ears. We are to live peacefully as good citizens in our lands as beacons of light in the darkness, although our laws and governance are not Christian. We must live out our faith as Jesus taught and lived, because this world is not our home.

THE MARRIAGE COVENANT

Although marriage is a gift from God, as a human institution it is open to the sin and corruption of the world. As God's covenant, the foundations for the union of man and woman is God ordained and sacred. Genesis 1 and 2 tells us that God created man, and because it was not good for him to be alone, God created woman to complement him. For this reason, a man leaves his parents and swears allegiance to his wife, and they become one flesh. Malachi 2:14 reinforces the institution of marriage, not only for individual couples but for God with Israel; God's declaration that "She is your companion and your wife by covenant" shows that marriage was originally instituted by God for his chosen people.

Men and women are spiritual equals before God (Galatians 3:28) and marriage a lifetime contract. This union of equals holds no room for misogynous thinking. God created males and females to fulfil union in each other through their commitment to God, and to each other, not in competition or subservience. God ordained marriage as a lifelong commitment, just as Jesus Christ's commitment to his church is forever.

INTIMACY OF HEART

On my third trip to Israel I visited the Beit Hatfutsot Museum of the Jewish People in Tel Aviv. This museum dedicated to the diaspora of Israel explains everything Jewish, including family, feasts, and traditions. A life-size display of a Jewish wedding ceremony moved me. Under a chuppah, or wedding canopy, the bride and groom stomp on a wine glass. Jewish custom includes the practice of the husband, and sometimes the wife, breaking a napkin-shrouded wine glass, usually after the seventh benediction, near the end of the ceremony. Before I saw this display, I knew of the practice of shouting "Mazel tov" around the glass-smashing at a Jewish wedding but it had little meaning. That day I felt a supernatural connection between my own spiritual life experiences and God's design for love and marriage, as described in the Bible.

Beit Hatfutsot Museum of the Jewish People, Tel Aviv, September 25, 2015

As the guide expounded on the significance of Jewish marriage, I felt God's love for me like never before. The enormity of January 2008 struck me, as I contrasted a shattered wine glass with the one I had at home in my cupboard, a carefully crafted work of art from God. When I arrived home, I investigated this Jewish glass-breaking tradition; various interpretations for the ancient ritual are based on customs and traditions from rabbis and the Talmud. The practice usually signifies the fragility of life, love, and our physical bodies, especially in light of the destruction of the Temple in AD 70. It is a sober reminder to temper our joy in light of all that may happen to us. "Serve the Lord with fear, and rejoice with trembling" (Psalm 2:11), words often used during the ritual, struck me forcefully as I recalled the emergence of two pieces, a broken heart, from an otherwise intact glass. I never fully realized the awe and majesty of God until that day when I recalled the strength of God's power to speak through the fragility of a glass.

I have learned that the answer to a broken heart is always God and his Word. Maybe God was admonishing my attitude toward the sign he had given me and he was reminding me to treat it with greater awe and respect. There in Tel Aviv I was convicted about not having done so. I wondered if this was my conscience, or God, speaking to me, but I knew I had to finish this book when I returned home.

God's heart cannot be smashed beyond repair. He is the source of all healing. The glass, which has no functional use, made me reflect even more on God's Word and what he was saying to me regarding my relationship with him. To his Church, the Bride, he is the Husband. My spiritual experience in Israel made me deeply reflect on what being Christian meant. Intimacy must not be cheapened by unfaithfulness in marriage or any kind of sexual sin, for those united in Christian marriage become one flesh as Christ and his church are one body. The bridegroom claims his bride in marriage just as Christ will one day claim his bride, the universal church. The marriage bed is sacred, as every Christian is the temple of the Holy Spirit.

Christians hold their marriages sacred for life and, despite weakness and temptation, they work to honor and protect their unions, and their spouses. I took my marriage vows seriously and was immensely blessed both times. Neither husband was perfect, just as I am not perfect. Both of my marriages grew to be healthy, intimate, and resilient through intimacy with God. This would not have been possible without knowing Jesus as Lord and Savior.

WALKING IN GOD'S INTENTIONAL INTIMACY

Christians intentionally following Christ and aiming to be Christ-like lights in this world must walk in intentional intimacy with God against the world. He sustains us when we stand on his Word. God made covenants with his people and held up those whose hearts were turned toward him. He knows his own. His will is in their hearts, as the prophet Jeremiah wrote:

> Behold, the days are coming, declares the Lord, when I will make a new covenant with the house of Israel and the house of Judah, not like the covenant that I made with their fathers on the day when I took them by the hand to bring them out of the land of Egypt, my covenant that they broke, though I was their husband, declares the Lord. But this is the covenant that I will make with the house of Israel after those days, declares the Lord: I will put my law within them and I will write it on their

hearts. And I will be their God and they shall be
my people. (Jeremiah 31:31–33)

We know that the love of God is greater than anything we can
experience in this world. Jeremiah emphasizes God's desire that his
law be within us and written on our hearts. God wants hearts like
David's, hearts after his own heart. He wants us to love what and
like he loves. We can only help others grow an intentional intimacy
with him and feel and return his love if our hearts are as he desires,
and there is no sin between us and him.

The world often admires Christ's fight for equality but ignores
his dislike of sin and corruption. Christians must learn from his
teachings and emulate his love. He was troubled by the hypocrisy
and dishonesty of the leadership of his day. As the Son of God he
did not come to replace God's laws and commandments but to fulfil
and teach them to the world, not just to the Jewish people. No one
can believe part of what Jesus said—it is all or nothing. The Bible is
either God's inspired Word or it is not. Similarly, there is no middle
ground with Christ: we are for him, or not. We will no longer ask
what God can do for us when we take up our cross and walk with
him. We will ask, and want to know, what God wants us to do for
him. When we truly love God, it is easier to defend all that he is,
because all that he is, we are striving to be also. There will be no
cherry picking, false flattery, emotionality, or casting a blind eye
to lesser sins as we self-righteously rail against what we see as more
serious ones.

Jesus taught honesty and love for all people, not shallow
and fleeting affection. He taught morals and values that were
countercultural but that challenged his followers to make a greater
commitment to his truth and courage. The people of his day had
never heard commands like only those who have no sin may cast the

first stone ([John 8:7], to those accusing the adulterer). The woman at the well was appalled that he would name her sin as he did, but Jesus loved her. Jesus loves women and men far beyond their love for their husbands or wives. He loves me far beyond any love I had for Corb or Stephen, my grandparents, father, mother, children, and grandchildren. Christ desires that everyone come to him. God calls us to imitate his love as his children and to walk in love as he loved us and gave himself for us. God desires that our love be like a fragrant offering, forever rising sweetly to him, requiring a genuine sacrifice on our part. Loving God as he requires costs much, but it is far more precious than all of the world's wealth—we are unable to fathom its vast worth.

INTIMACY GOD'S WAY

If we live for God and follow his Word, and trust the constancy of his love, we can differentiate between the love of the world and the love of God. God created love and relationships but *his* love is based in truth. True intimacy with God comes when our hearts are fully turned toward him. To comprehend that God alone fully knows me and loves me, despite my flaws, is an epiphany. That he loves me and wants me to be emotionally, physically, intellectually, and spiritually whole is amazing. I must study and remember his teachings, primarily through the Bible but also through prayer in the power of the Holy Spirit.

I understand why some people give everything, even their whole lives, to be truly loved by someone who will love them in return. I have come as close to this, as is humanly possible, twice in my life. Yet relationships with others do not come close to the relationship and identity I have with God through Jesus. Human relationships did not satisfy Noah, Moses, David, or Christ's apostles, either.

Marilyn O. Flower

Our love for others is not forced or coerced when the love of God is within our hearts but is genuine, true, and sincere. An outpouring of godly love flows from the hearts of God's own to others. It is not gushy, filled with pretense, smothering, or overbearing. I can go nowhere to escape God's presence. Wherever I go, he is there. Even more important, I have no desire to escape God's great intentional love for me, and I desire to intentionally love him as he desires.

CHAPTER 9

S: SANCTIFICATION PROCEEDING

Sanctify them in the truth; your word is truth.
(John 17:17)

Christians live in the world, yet are not of it. As they are obedient to God's call, they are drawn closer to him and further from the world. No believer can serve two masters: he or she cannot be God's child and serve him and simultaneously be a slave of the world.

Believers are sanctified in the truth of God's Word, yet this will not make living in the world easier, even with his Spirit indwelling us. The world is an alluring place, but it is not our home. When we follow Jesus and want to model our lives by his teachings, changes happen that unsettle what once was our world. God loves us too much to allow us to continue in brokenness when he knows that we are focused on him and seek his guidance to make our hearts more like his. God commands us to be completely new beings. Gradually each day we are transformed more and more to resemble Christ.

JUSTIFICATION, SANCTIFICATION, AND GLORIFICATION

Justification, sanctification, and glorification have been preached down through the ages; circumcision has not. None of these are complicated when the Bible is our guide. As I meditated on several passages pertaining to salvation (also called justification or positional sanctification), including Ephesians 2:4–5, I pondered my own salvation as a child. Nothing I did, or could ever do on my own and in my own strength, brought me salvation and freedom from eternal separation from God. Salvation, being saved or born again, through faith in Jesus by God's grace, is a gift I was given as I accepted Jesus into my heart as my Lord. Without believing in Jesus's death on the cross, we are not worthy to be in God's presence. With it, we, the unjust, are declared just before a righteous judge. Jesus atones for our sin. Justification, however, is the beginning of life in Christ—not the fulfilment of it.

Since I have been born again, I have lived to fulfil God's call on my life as his adopted child. I have worked hard, constantly battling my will, and always sinning, struggling to be obedient to God's will, as the Bible teaches. This second and present phase, called progressive or experiential sanctification, includes being separated from the world and set apart for God.

Progressive sanctification will be part of my life until I die, or until Jesus comes, which will bring glorification, complete and ultimate sanctification for eternity. God's gracious lovingkindness and mercy toward me, through the power and guidance of the Holy Spirit, have sustained me, not solely to steady me but holding me up straight so that I may grow closer to him. I am only now coming to a place in my sanctification where I can truly enjoy life as a daughter of the King. Living for him, while living in this world, is what God wants.

TENSION: THE WORLD VERSUS GOD'S LOVE AND LAWS

God's love and his laws are perfect and holy, as he is holy. There was no tension between his love and his laws before sin entered the world. Christians are called to be holy, to live with the tension every day of demonstrating the love of God and living as he commands, according to his ways, which include his laws.

Jesus forgives our sin, but he does not give believers a license to sin. A circumcised heart loves God's unchanging ways, laws, and truth. When we are justified, our hearts circumcised, and we are being sanctified, we understand how and why there may be tension within us, and between us and others, as we have the love of God in us while we live in a world opposed to his truth. We uphold God's truth in love as our circumcised hearts are guided and empowered by the Holy Spirit.

After the division of the twelve tribes of Israel into ten in the northern region of Israel and two in the southern region of Judah, around 933–930 BC, there was much unrest and struggle between the kings and prophets over God's laws and commandments, sometimes civilly between kingdoms, and later, war and destruction from outside. When kings and prophets held the people accountable to God's ways, life was relatively peaceful; when the king erred, destruction was imminent. For Israel, who never could be faithful to God, the end came through the pharaoh of Egypt and the Assyrians in 722 BC. Judah's end came when Babylon's king Nebuchadnezzar defeated them in 586 BC. God wanted his people to love and obey him, but they drew further from him. Israel had been an unfaithful wife and God used Israel's and Judah's enemies to defeat them.

The Old Testament has no happy ending; the Israelites kept wallowing in sin, defeated from within and without. Their hope of a Messiah to give them a better existence on earth, spoken of hundreds of times by the prophets, especially Isaiah, was and is not what they thought it would be. They sought a man like King David. Most did not recognize Jesus as their Messiah. But Jesus was the sprout from Jesse's rod, as predicted by the prophets.

READINESS OF HEART

Each day brings an opportunity to learn something new, if we intentionally listen. It is easier to stick with the familiar, especially as we age. For years I partially listened to God, while trying to please people. Being willing to set aside our own agendas for his calls for a new perspective. As we live each day for ourselves, it is easy to get lost in the temporal and forget about the God who made us, especially if he has not always been a priority in our lives. Even when disaster strikes, we may not turn to him first unless someone helps us see him. It is only when God draws nonbelievers to himself or the Holy Spirit helps believers see the error of their ways that hearts are readied to change.

Through all of our circumstances, God can create the desire within us to want to change, but the decision is ours, the direction matters, the focus of learning is important, and the condition of our hearts is all-important. Appeasing him and receiving what he could give them was what the Israelites wanted; knowing him was not their first priority. They reverted to their pagan ways when hardships arose. Like many of us, they wanted their needs met. Moses may have wanted to please God, but he was not holy enough, according to God's measure.

Jesus offers new life to everyone who will follow him. But we must listen to his Word and to the Holy Spirit. People must listen well—not a common strength today. Circumcision occurs in a person's soul at salvation. The circumcised heart knows that what is of God is what matters. The affirmation coming from God, not man, is most valuable to those who love him first. Once we are saved or justified and our heart circumcised, we want to spend our lives growing more like Jesus in holiness, righteousness, and love.

We know God desires a two-way relationship. Justification and circumcision are God's work due to our faith when our hearts are ready, but progressive sanctification is our work, although Father, Son, and Holy Spirit help and guide us through God's Word. Readiness of heart is also essential to our sanctification. We must want to be sanctified just as we wanted to be saved. We must grow in our faith in relation to what God desires. This is not to say that God will not intervene in our circumstances through other people, and in our lives to change us, but he will not force himself on anyone. We have free will until we die.

IMPERFECT AND DESIRING CHANGE

Being given the gift of eternal life is the beginning of relationship with God. A follower of Christ is a new being but believers are still imperfect. Some sin may take a while to defeat or keep under control, if ever. Persons become like Abraham, David, or Martha, seeking the heart of God, trying to be obedient to his will, and trusting him. Although believers will still sin, sin no longer holds the attraction it once did. The Bible reminds us that everyone who makes a practice of sinning also practices lawlessness. We know Jesus came to take away sin, and in him there is no sin, but if he had not upheld the law, he himself would have sinned. No one who abides in Jesus habitually sins, as Christ's perfection shows up sin. If we remain as the Israelites, wandering and searching after what God can do for us, following Christ may lose its appeal. We will soon follow familiar idols and habits. God cannot be fooled. We either want him, or what he can provide.

I know I can never be holy and righteous as God is, but the Holy Spirit convicts me of my sin. Although I am remorseful, I still do not do what is right. My heart is changed, and is changing, but I will always be imperfect in this imperfect body. Those who continue in their old ways do not know God as he desires to be known, and as he teaches in the Bible. A heart that has undergone the sword of circumcision wants to know what grieves God so that it can be avoided. A believer knows he or she is imperfect but desires to change and become as Christ-like as possible. The intention of the heart is changed to a new level of purity that only God knows.

The concept of once-saved always-saved may make for good discussion, but it detracts from studying God's Word, spreading the gospel, and serving others. God alone knows who is his. They follow after him. Like David, when believers sin, they repent and return, even more determined to follow after God's heart. In our imperfection, and convicted about what is sinful, believers seek God's help by allowing the Holy Spirit to sanctify them into the image of Christ. We desire, and need, the Holy Spirit to root out the decay and filth in our human hearts that harbor the perversion and corruption of the world.

THE SWORD OF GOD

One of the greatest and most surprising parts of my new-found understanding of God and his Word is how he purposely changes us through his Word. My heart is constantly being sanctified through the Bible as the Holy Spirit helps me sift through my thoughts and intentions. I should never be surprised by the enormity of what God can and does do, but I am. I am overwhelmed by the hand of God on my life, not only on it, but in it.

> For the Word of God is living and active, sharper than any two-edged sword, piercing to the division of soul and of spirit, of joints and of marrow, and discerning the thoughts and intentions of the heart. And no creature is hidden from his sight, but all are naked and exposed to the eyes of him to whom we must give account. (Hebrews 4:12–13)

The Bible is the most powerful book in the world, but it has taken me many years and much pain to learn this. God's sword of the spirit discerns every thought and intention of the heart. We are wise to welcome God's gift of personal spiritual discernment.

Our sinful, selfish selves are put to death as we begin to live a new life in Jesus Christ. Some of this happens almost instantaneously, some slowly. The Bible is the answer and the guide to leaving the broken person behind and taking on a new personhood. Partly new, however, will not suffice; a true Christian is fully Christian. Being rebirthed into a child of God will only happen when we are ready.

Every day I allow God to take charge of my life. Gradually I reached the point of accepting the glass as God's revealing himself to me. Those two pieces of glass and the glass itself are a sign of God's faithfulness, unending love, listening ear, concern, and broken heart—a tangible sign from an unseen God who calls me to further sanctification and softening of my heart until I die, or Jesus returns. My heart had to be opened fully to his Word before I could even understand the significance of the glass.

All things happen in God's time, not ours. This is particularly hard for those of us who are impatient, but God is helping me with that too. Much has happened in my life after this life-changing incident. Despite many trials, my faith in God continues to grow, and except to share my story several times, I rarely look at the broken glass in the cabinet. The memory of how it came to be is deeply etched in my heart. God's visible sign is real but it is also mystery, in addition to being miraculous. Only God can explain it.

A CIRCUMCISED HEART

i. Has said yes to Jesus

With Jesus in our lives, we are no longer in the dark. The darker the place we are in, however, the greater we see the light of Christ when our hearts are open and pliable. Our lives can no longer be the same once we are Christ's. I cannot thread a needle, find something in a cupboard, or read a book in the dark. But with a light, even a flickering candle, I can. In full light, I can use my senses and be informed. It is the same with knowing Jesus. When we become his, we see as for the first time. As we become more Christ-like, we understand more of what he requires of his followers and we are more fully focused on him and his Word.

ii. Is dead to self

Once I knew that I was God's, through Christ, I saw that everything that I did outside of his will pained him. I did not want to disobey God. I could no longer engage in those things which he found grievous, and I wanted to separate myself from sin. As Paul writes in Romans 7, however, as much as I try, I still do what I do not wish to do. I sin. God knows my sincerity when I repent. My desire is to die to myself and serve God with the awe and fear owed him, while rejoicing in the mightiness of his love and power.

iii. Has tension with the world

Death to ourselves and new life in Christ equates to tension with the world. Giving birth and dying are usually painful processes. The same is true of dying to oneself. Sometimes it is the death of habits and relationships, but it may be the birth of new habits and new relationships. New life in him is free to all who call upon his name. The joy of new life in Christ far outweighs the cost of any loss of turning from an old way of living to a new one.

iv. Still experiences the pain of sin

After salvation it may be possible to wander away from God, to be angry with him or disillusioned. Some believe that wandering away after salvation affects only the rewards received in heaven; others, the consequences are more severe. The Bible states that land that has drunk the rain and produces a crop useful to those for whose sake it is cultivated receives a blessing from God. But if it bears thorns and thistles, it is worthless and near to being cursed, and its end is to be burned. This is a warning to us to guard what Christ has given us lest it be whisked away by the enemy. There is no certainty we can or will ever be retrieved again, once lost. I am thankful that God beckoned me back to him those times that I wandered. Each time I returned through the power and strength of the Holy Spirit, I became stronger in him and his Word, but it took much effort on my part.

v. Hungers and thirsts for righteousness

Jesus is the only source of thirst-quenching, living water. As the woman at the well was changed because she knew that what Jesus had told her was true, we too must believe what the Bible tells us about him because it is also true. If we do not believe the Word of God, we do not have Jesus, the source. Believing is the first step. After that comes hungering and thirsting for righteousness. Jesus is the living water that will quench our thirst. We seek God and find him, as the cross of Jesus bridges the chasm between us and God.

Headwaters of the Jordan, the largest of four,
in Tel Dan, Israel, February 9, 2012

vi. Is separate and set apart for God

When God spoke to the Israelites through Moses, he demanded that they be separated from other people groups according to where they lived and whom they married. This would keep them from sinful, idolatrous behavior and set them apart for himself. Faithful Bible-believing Christians will work hard to keep God's commandments. God provides patience and self-control to obey his will when the heart is ready, and he is asked. Paul reminds us of the importance of walking by the Spirit so that we do not seek to satisfy our bodies. If we walk by the Spirit, we will find love, joy, peace, patience, kindness, goodness, faithfulness, gentleness, and self-control; these will identify us as Christians and draw others to want to know more about Christ.

> For the desires of the flesh are against the Spirit, and the desires of the Spirit are against the flesh, for these are opposed to each other, to keep you from doing the things you want to do ... But the fruit of the Spirit is love, joy, peace, patience, kindness, goodness, faithfulness, gentleness, self-control, against such things there is no law. And those who belong to Christ Jesus have crucified the flesh with its passions and desires. If we live by the Spirit, let us also walk with the Spirit. (Galatians 5:17, 22–25)

vii. Is united with others in Christ

Obedience to God's Word brings a joy that is not possible with any other obedience. This softens the heart to hear God's voice, causing us to love others as he loves them. Sanctification is transformation. As Jesus said to those who believed him, "If you abide in my word, you are truly my disciples, and you will know the truth, and the truth will set you free" (John 8:31–32). When we trust only in him and allow him to be Lord of our lives, we fear nothing. We are free. The mark of a totally committed Christian is how much he or she loves God and his Word.

There is a fellowship of biblically faithful Christians throughout the world united in Christ. These people make up the church of Jesus Christ and they treasure God's Word. As believers allow God to sanctify them in the truth of his Word, his will will unfold perfectly, but only he knows how this will be done. Jesus is the way, the Word made flesh; the Bible is the Word, the procedural manual.

> If we say we have fellowship with him while we walk in darkness, we lie and do not practice the truth. But if we walk in the light, as he is in the light, we have fellowship with one another, and the blood of Jesus his Son cleanses us from all sin. If we say we have no sin, we deceive ourselves, and the truth is not in us. If we confess our sins, He is faithful and just to forgive us our sins and to cleanse us from all unrighteousness. If we say we have not sinned, we make him a liar and his word is not in us. (1 John 1:6–10)

Job knew that the fear of God was wisdom and turning away from evil was understanding. Some Christians feel that God dealt harshly with the righteous Job, but the book of Job has much to teach us. Christians are united in Christ by their love for God and his Word, and their seeking righteousness, not by any holiness that they may claim. God's perfect justice is not to be questioned.

SANCTIFICATION

Some religious debates involve words being bandied about without the debaters giving much thought or study to the underlying concepts. Many of these cannot be relegated to either extremes of liberal or conservative, fundamentalist/legalist or revisionist, literal or figurative. Any debate can only be valid when those of alternative viewpoints open-mindedly study and read the other side's viewpoints. Fear enters when people are afraid to read opposing viewpoints. Most third-world theologians are well informed about Western theology, yet the reverse is not true. Belief in God is too important to dismiss by following the culture and not examining all viewpoints, especially God's Word. It would be wise to know and understand to whom we give our allegiance.

> But understand this, that in the last days there will come times of difficulty. For people will be lovers of self, lovers of money, proud, arrogant, abusive, disobedient to their parents, ungrateful, unholy, heartless, unappeasable, slanderous, without self-control, brutal, not loving good, treacherous, reckless, swollen with conceit, lovers of pleasure rather than lovers of God, having the appearance of godliness, but denying its power. Avoid such people. For among them are those who creep into households and capture weak women, burdened with sins and led astray by various passions, always learning and never able to arrive at a knowledge of the truth. (2 Timothy 3:1–7)

Those who believe they are holy and righteous because they claim to be believers and adopt a holier-than-thou attitude are mistaken. We can never be as holy or righteous as God, no matter how hard we strive. Even some Christians have difficulty understanding God's holiness, immanence, and immutability because they have trouble understanding and relating to a being with qualities they cannot possess. Today mystery, the unknown, intrigue, and even danger, are not only accepted, but welcomed, while the complexity and mystery of God is often seen as irrelevant.

Friendship with the world is enmity with God, according to the Bible. This biblical concept troubles some who may have difficulty reconciling their faith with their lives. God's Word is clear, however: sin is missing the mark and both malicious behavior and evil are not qualities God wants in his children. God abhors sin. He always forgives when we repent with sincere, humble hearts. God wants us to be at peace with everyone, while working hard to be more Christ-like. This can only be achieved with the Holy Spirit's convicting us and guiding our paths, progressively sanctifying us until death.

WISDOM OF THE HEART

My hunger to understand the entire Bible came at the point in my spiritual transformation when God opened the eyes of my heart to the necessity of reading all of it. I now identify with Jesus's conversation with Mary sitting at his feet and Martha the homemaker who was distraught that Mary did not help her in the kitchen (Luke 10). I identify with both women, but now the Mary portion of me has taken over. My favorite pastime is sitting at the feet of Jesus, listening to God's Word and contemplating its meaning.

To the world knowledge is power. Some, obsessed with acquiring it, however, do not differentiate it from wisdom. Although we may strive to learn everything, it is impossible to know everything and less possible to be wise about all we know at the same time. God is the source of knowledge and wisdom, and he provides discernment to all who ask. We must ask God to teach us his paths, treasure his commandments, and be attentive to his Word so that we discern his will.

If we cry out to God for wisdom, searching for it as for hidden treasures, we will understand more of him. Our lives take unexpected twists and turns. We may never know what circumstances were the consequences of our own actions. All we know is that God works even the worst parts of our lives together for our spiritual growth. I have grown best and found him more when I sought him in my darkest days. My perspective on the major issues of life— death, dying, family, marriage, giving birth, child raising—have changed completely because of reading the Bible, something I never anticipated.

My desire is that those I love would read the Bible and come to a saving knowledge of Jesus Christ. God calls us not to believe what others say without questioning it. We must look for ourselves, experiencing the living Word of God, testing its pages, allowing the words to speak into our hearts. As the roots of a tree grow deep in the soil searching for water and nutrients, I long to be understood, to be nurtured, and to be cared for by God. In difficult times I longed for authentic meaning, deep love, and sincere compassion, just as the parched branches on a vine display its leaves seeking the warmth of the sun by day and the soothing balm of dewdrops by evening. Relief from heartache, and spiritual growth, came because of my pain. God heard the suffering in my heart. He works his will so lovingly and patiently through our adversity and provides the wisdom we require to grow closer to him.

God's truth brings healing and freedom as his Word sanctifies us. If our faith is important to us and we see how far we fall short of God's command to love as he loves, we know we need his sanctifying grace. God's Word has the power to unite all of his children. God sanctifies my eyes. He wants me to see as he sees so that I may see others as he sees them. With the Holy Spirit's guidance, I pray that my ears are open to hear all that God wants me to hear, not only to hear but also to listen and understand. I pray that God sanctifies my hands to do the work that he wants me to do and my feet to go where and how he wants me to go. I pray that God continues to sanctify me to be the daughter he desires that I be.

CHAPTER 10

E: ETERNAL EXPECTATIONS

> There is neither Jew nor Greek, there is neither
> slave nor free, there is no male and female, for you
> are all one in Christ Jesus. And if you are Christ's,
> then you are Abraham's offspring, heirs according
> to promise. (Galatians 3:28–29)

I am God's daughter. I have been redeemed, bought with Jesus's blood and righteousness. I have a sure and certain expectation of resurrection and eternity with Jesus.

PROMISE AND EXPECTATION

When God created humans, he did not intend for them to live for seventy years and then be forever gone. We were created for fellowship with God for eternity, yet, like Adam, Eve, and the people of Moses's day, we turn our hearts from him. When we turn to God in faith, we desire his will and we learn to be obedient to him. We cannot see God's face but we can behold his glory through Jesus. Through Jesus the Holy Spirit changes our hearts and frees us from death and sin. Gradually through the sanctifying grace of God we are transformed into the likeness of his Son for eternity.

EXPECT TO QUESTION

The world is almost split on the question "Is this life all there is?" Much of the West believes it is. Others believe that after death everyone goes to heaven. They base this on their feelings and what the world tells them, not on what God reveals in the Bible. Popular culture believes that we cannot absolutely know anything; therefore, we can be sure of nothing: we can be sure that we can be absolutely sure of nothing. This type of philosophical discourse once intrigued me.

In 1983 I did a course titled "The Philosophical and Psychological Foundations of Science Education" at Memorial University. It caused me to wonder how someone across the street at the Health Sciences Centre, depending upon the knowledge of experts in cancer care to provide treatment, and give them hope of beating their disease, might respond to what sometimes is viewed as nonsensical metaphysical jargon. If nothing can be known, we are lost; we become totally confused, mentally unstable, delusional, or worse. A few months later that year, Corb was diagnosed with cancer, and my thoughts generated by that course became our reality. Corb and I listened to medical knowledge espoused by our healthcare providers, but we knew that God was in charge of the outcome, as difficult as it might get. Science is not the enemy. It is a gift from God. But worship of it, or of anything outside God, is.

EXPECT TO BE KNOWN BY YOUR FRUITS

We can be confident in knowing that, if we live as faithful Christian witnesses, our faith will not only be known in this life but the spiritual fruit of our labor will also be passed on, as it was with my grandmother, great-uncle, Corb, Stephen, and Abraham Ulrikab. We are known by our fruits. It is comforting to know that God can use us to help someone find the narrow gate. The Bible attests to fruits passed on through the ages that will be known for eternity. The metaphor of vines, trees, and fruit representing humanity and its good and bad choices run throughout all of God's Word. Jesus is the true vine, and we are his branches. When we grow out of Jesus, and are rooted in God's word, we will bear much good fruit.

The books of Kings, Chronicles, and the prophets largely describe the conditions during the divided kingdoms of Judah and Israel. They are also rich with wisdom to help us become more obedient followers of Christ. One popular passage is the metaphor of the potter and the clay:

> The word that came to Jeremiah from the LORD: "Arise, and go down to the potter's house, and there I will let you hear my words." So I went down to the potter's house, and there he was working at his wheel. And the vessel he was making of clay was spoiled in the potter's hand, and he reworked it into another vessel, as it seemed good to the potter to do. (Jeremiah 18:1–4)

The clay, spoiled in the potter's hands, had to be reworked. The spoiled vessel of Israel and Judah did not heed God's voice through either the kings or the prophets. They were hard-hearted and wicked, worshipping what God had forbidden. We often are like spoiled clay in God's hands, when we too ignore God's voice.

God repeatedly entreated the Israelites to return to him. But because they chose paganism over him, he gave them over to their sinful lusts. All of Israel's kings were evil, while Judah had several kings who were better than most, in addition to several good and great kings. Despite the warnings and pleas of the faithful prophets, Israel and Judah ultimately rejected God. Josiah of Judah tried to be obedient to God, loving him with all of his heart, but it was too late for the nation and for him. Today some question whether we are again at a point in history where it is too late for a small and faithful remnant to turn the tide of history and the faith of nations. The Bible entreats believers to have a heart like Josiah's, so that in following God we will produce good fruit, giving us expectation of eternity with him.

The Old Testament is necessary for our understanding and appreciation of the New Testament. King Josiah, Daniel, Esther, Job, and Ruth encourage us today, especially those who are being persecuted for their faith, enabling them to face dark days with the joy of the Lord.

ALL ARE CALLED

All were invited to the wedding feast in one of Jesus's parables. But not all chose to go, because not all were ready. Faith in God is open to everyone, but not all will accept. Some will totally reject him; some are not ready to accept him. Jesus's parables in the New Testament echo the stories of Israel in the Old Testament. Most of God's faithful Old Testament leaders had difficulty with their followers; they were selfish, stubborn, and disobedient people, just as we are.

Nonbelievers and skeptics of our day resemble many of the Jewish people of the first century; they did not accept Jesus as Messiah when he was on earth or as the church grew. The apostles and those they commissioned proclaimed the gospel to the whole world, but still many refused to believe. A good life in the here and now is not what the good news of the New Testament brings; expectation of eternal life is.

Before Corb died we compromised sometimes on what we preferred to do, because we could not be sure that elderly family members would be around for the next important event. Surprisingly, the elderly family members outlived Corb. We were frugal out of necessity to pay on student loans and our mortgage. Our student loans were paid off the month before Corb's death. People live this way because most people do not get sick and die in their early thirties. There are, however, no guarantees that our lives will continue indefinitely or that they will be healthy or enjoyable, but many do live as if this is the case. We will all die. While we are alive, we all live in expectation of something—a peaceful old age, being able to enjoy grandchildren or a warmer climate, or reminisce with pictures and movies of the good old days. Christians, however, are sure of a far greater existence—eternal life in heaven with a perfect body.

EXPECT THE UNEXPECTED

In early February 2009, after a spiritual retreat brought me back to theological reflection and writing, I ruminated briefly on the glass, which had been out of my sight but not my mind for a year. I remained silent, although I felt God speaking to me. I discerned a call to ordained ministry but struggled with being a part of the institutional church. I questioned my lack of faith at a time when God had graced me with an overwhelming symbol of his love. I wondered, had I been disrespectful of God, a poor listener, or was it not yet God's time for whatever-was-to-be? I knew that God is perfectly patient and understanding. God knew me and loved me, despite my flaws, and if he had purpose for the glass, he would reveal it to me.

The glass made me seek the character of God. I realized that if I relied on my life circumstances and emotions, I could define God's character to fit *my* desires of who he should be. But I am not God, and the Bible is the only source of all truth. The glass contravened nothing of God's Word. It had no special or secret knowledge. It was simply God's reassurance and encouragement at a difficult time in my life and a trying time in my church's history when the Bible was again being challenged and threatened.

Through the Bible God lets us know how much he loves us. We learn that he desires that we pattern our hearts after his. God sought David to replace Saul because God knew David's heart, even though later he had sinned grievously. David was humble, faithful, and obedient to God, because he loved God's laws and repented of his sin. Psalm 51 shows that David loved God, depended on him, trusted him, and was convicted by his conscience after the prophet Nathan confronted him of his sin with Bathsheba to turn his heart toward God and to seek his mercy. David's raw emotion, his pain, and his subsequent repentance make many of the psalms comforting and reassuring to us in our own pain. We see God in action through David's eyes and heart. God knows we will sin, but he also knows that hearts turned to him, patterning after his, as David's did, will sin less.

The eyes of my heart opened as I realized how precious and instructive all of God's words are. As I meditated more on the Bible, I realized that every one of God's thoughts and deeds are mighty, awesome, and true, not myth, as some teach. Both the Old and New Testaments are God's inspired Word. I began to understand that the entire Bible is a deep and intricate account of God's story. I understood that my sign in the glass was literally a breath from the Holy Spirit, and it caused me to humbly draw closer to God and the Bible.

EXPECTATION: A NEW HEART

God desires all hearts to be circumcised. Circumcision of the heart is an intimate process between each believer and God. It involves God's cutting out the unhealthy, undesired parts of our hearts by his sword so that we are new creations. The circumcised heart no longer has the propensity to harbor infection, or sin. It is changed, but still human and open to sin.

Christians no longer hold the Jewish tradition of a day of rest on the Sabbath as God mandated Israel to do; Jesus *is* the Sabbath. Most Christians' day of remembrance, the first day of the week, Sunday, celebrates resurrection, hope, and new life. Our Christian fellowship and congregating together is for worship, praise, and celebration of all that God has done for us, a remembering, not a reenactment, of Jesus's completed perfect sacrifice. Likewise, we are not saved by following God's laws, but we desire to follow them because we have new hearts—hearts fashioned after his—like David's, although not many will seek his heart to the extent that David did. Only God knows how much each human heart seeks after him.

God could have given up on humanity in the times of Noah, Sodom and Gomorrah, or Moses and the Israelites as they left Egypt and aimlessly wandered for forty years. How gracious and loving God is to not have given up on us. Like the Israelites we too have difficulty understanding God and his Word, but with circumcised hearts we know inwardly what is of him. We love his Word, but we must battle our flesh to uphold it.

There is absolutely nothing new under the sun; one only need read the Old Testament books of the kings and prophets to see that this is so. It is a matter of degree. People's struggles have always been between wanting their way and obeying God's will. All around us the devil entices us to be selfish and encourages us to fall further from God's will and glory. His aim is for our hearts to become hardened so that we are unable to discern God's will, that we, like pharaoh, will harden our own hearts so that eventually God hardens our hearts even further. The Bible repeatedly warns of the dangers of straying from God's ways, although we may have found Jesus, the narrow gate.

God continuously calls us back, but repeatedly we refuse. We do not know how long God will continue to call us back, or how many more chances we will have. The Bible teaches that there is a limit to God's mercy and that he alone is perfectly just. He may even use others' evil against us. Ultimately God will give the world over to its selfish desires.

The Old Testament's stories help us understand God and the human condition. Understanding the Bible is the only way we can understand us and the gospel of Jesus Christ, because we cannot begin to understand him, his ministry, and his call on our lives, without first understanding the Old Testament he taught from.

LEARNING GOD'S WAY

The Bible is the supreme Word of God, as God says it is. Only God can save us from our own depravity. Everything else must be measured against his Word. God saved me from a life of self-pity, bitterness, and anger by leading me through Jesus, the only well that forever quenches thirst to read the entire Bible.

Religion and faith are not synonymous. Dependence on traditions, rituals, doctrine, and dogma do not equal a relationship with the triune God. Paul was concerned that followers of Christ would be deceived as Eve had been by Satan's cunning deceptions and led astray from a total devotion to God. We, also, must be aware of the cunning deceptions in this day. The Holy Spirit and knowing the Bible help us guard our hearts against such things.

I see three errors of understanding regarding salvation and expectation of heaven within the Christian faith. First, the belief Stephen first likened to a vaccine or an inoculation. Some believe that if a person is baptized into a church then he or she is saved eternally through the sacrament of baptism, and, as long as the person abides by prescribed church rules, how he or she lives does not matter. Because that person has been inoculated, then he or she is saved and free from error, including being free from the teaching of erroneous doctrine. This way of understanding elevates church doctrine and denies the power of the cross, of God's Word, and of the Holy Spirit. Salvation, unless on a deathbed or at the twelfth hour, will result in a change of life, never perfection—but always good fruit—as we are indwelled by the Holy Spirit. Only Jesus can say if the inoculation was effective. Inoculation means receiving just a minute amount of an antigen, preventing an onslaught by the virus itself; vaccinations are sometimes not only ineffective but they can also be deadly in themselves. Stephen's concern was that inoculation could prevent a person from hearing the full truth of the gospel as that person had a false sense of security.

Second, salvation as an insurance policy: the contract one has with God guarantees heaven and any trial or disaster will be taken care of automatically by God, because the saved are his, nothing can touch them. If a believer has hardship and it is not corrected through prayer, it is assumed that either that person does not know God or did not pray in a proper manner. Such erroneous thinking dismisses all persecuted Christians and martyrs as unsaved. Just as faithful believers in the Bible did not have everything go right in their lives, many Christians experience trials and hardships, sometimes more often and severe than nonbelievers do. Jesus does not assure a good life, free from persecution. He said, in fact, that if we follow him we are sure to have troubles (Matthew 10:22; John 16:33).

And, third, salvation is personal, to keep to oneself. Our faith, if it is genuine, is not to be kept to ourselves. A Christian must share his or her faith with others, gently and lovingly, never compromising God's Word, as salvation is the greatest gift of life. A Christian's life will also be his or her witness.

WITNESS AND SERVICE

Eternal life with Christ is ours through salvation, but we must also expect changes in our lives as we are made more pliable to hear, understand, love, and share God's Word with all honesty to a broken, sinful, and messy world. We can expect to have our share of trials and heartaches, but we take solace in the knowledge that we will never have to handle them ourselves. The greatest blessing that we have as Christians is the hope that others will turn to Christ for salvation as we witness to them. This world greatly needs good news. We must work heartily for God and not for people because we serve God, not man. Allowing God to use us as vessels to bring Jesus and the Bible to others is a great privilege and honor.

I have always been fascinated by the stories of missionaries who give selflessly of themselves in faraway lands. Most nations in the world would never know Jesus or have copies of the Bible if it were not for brave and devout people like the Moravian missionaries who came to Greenland and Labrador in the 1700s. Many native people had rich full lives in Christ because of the Gospel's lovingly being passed to them by God's faithful servants. During the colonial period the Bible was more often than not brought by missionaries, not colonizers or governors.

One group of five young American missionary families who

traveled in the 1950s to the Amazon in Ecuador, connecting with a primitive and isolated tribe, inspires me. Five faithful husbands and fathers were brutally murdered by Waodani warriors when they landed their small Mission Aviation Fellowship aircraft into the jungle to make contact with the natives. They did not shoot the natives, because they knew the Waodani were not saved. As a testament to their faith and hope of eternal life, their families remained in Ecuador after the tragedy, lived among the Waodani, forgave them, and brought many of them to eternal life in Christ. This true story, filled with love, joy, and expectation, was the basis for the extraordinary documentary "Beyond the Gates of Splendor" (2005) and the movie "The End of the Spear" (2006).

Over the years many courageous Christian witnesses have ventured out of their comfort zones and into areas not only of poverty but also of violence and brutality to spread the good news of Jesus Christ. They were aware of the call upon their lives as his followers, but they never knew how their lives would unfold or end. They did, however, know their Father and where they would spend eternity. Although their witness may have cost them their lives, their expectation of eternal life could never be taken from them.

Christian martyrs of the past, and those imprisoned today, fought for their lives while spreading God's message of hope and redemption. Many faithful Christian missionaries today risk their lives to distribute Bibles while also providing clean drinking water, food, and shelter in countries where Christians are imprisoned and sometimes killed for their beliefs. They give their physical lives so that others may have better earthly lives and an eternity with Jesus.

Not Expecting an Easy Life

> Put on the whole armor of God that you may be
> able to stand against the schemes of the devil. For
> we do not wrestle against flesh and blood, but
> against the rulers, against the authorities, against
> the cosmic powers over this present darkness,
> against the spiritual forces of evil in the heavenly
> places. Therefore take up the whole armor of God
> that you may be able to withstand in the evil day,
> and having done all, to stand firm. Stand therefore,
> having fastened on the belt of truth, and having put
> on the breastplate of righteousness, and, as shoes for
> your feet, having put on the readiness given by the
> gospel of peace. In all circumstances take up the
> shield of faith, with which you can extinguish all the
> flaming darts of the evil one; and take the helmet
> of salvation, and the sword of the Spirit, which is
> the word of God, praying at all times in the Spirit,
> with all prayer and supplication. To that end keep
> alert with all perseverance, making supplication for
> all the saints ... (Ephesians 6:11–18)

Hundreds of sermons have been written on the need to put on
the full armor of God, but nothing compares to actually reading
Ephesians 6 aloud. Because of the adversities in my life, I have
learned to cry out to God, praying for wisdom, understanding, and
discernment in a world that believes there is no absolute truth. I have
pored over God's Word. I struggled with my call to the priesthood
after Stephen's death. By then I looked at the glass differently. God's
sign to me drove me deeper into his Word. Visiting Israel and leading

an in-depth Bible study gave me a greater understanding of God's story and solidified God's call to ministry.

NO FEAR

As Christians we should not fear or worry; Jesus told us he would never leave us (Hebrews 13:5b). With Jesus, our hope for the future is secure. One indication of salvation is the way a person approaches impending death. Although there may be concern over pain management, leaving loved ones, or even loss of dignity, most believers do not fear death. They anticipate seeing Jesus and reuniting with loved ones who also believed, which is comforting for those dying and in mourning, and being relieved from worldly suffering and anguish.

Our salvation guarantees the kingdom of God in heaven—freedom from the second death. The Bible teaches much about heaven and hell, but these are not popular topics today. There is the popular heaven and hell genre of novels and movies, some of which claim to be Bible-based, but little of sound teaching. All believers are free to study the Bible on their own, however, and some of them do. God works in the minds and hearts of his people despite the sin of their leaders.

I was reminded of the importance of the assurance of salvation and God's being in total control of everything one evening as I watched a commercial for a cancer care facility. Several people in the commercial said, in effect, "Well, I'm still here, aren't I?" When both of my husbands were dying of cancer, I would have done almost anything to keep them alive. I read and researched everything, but I would, however, never have done anything to jeopardize their, or my, spiritual well-being. Medical science helped ease Corb's and

Stephen's pain, but chemotherapy likely decreased their lifespan. I cannot imagine having dealt with their illnesses without God, yet I know there are worse things than death: the most serious of all is not knowing him. The commercial prompted me to recall Stephen's response each morning, near the end of his life, as he awoke: "Well, I'm still here." His faith was sure; he was ready to leave. As Christians, with eternity awaiting us, we should embrace heaven as we face the end of our lives. Earlier that week Stephen had given yet another sermon to a family member about what really mattered in life, commenting on not having his wallet in his pocket. I thought of all who fight terminal illness to stay alive, and I did both times with Corb and Stephen, versus the deliberate surrender of a soul to God. These priorities change with time and circumstances. Stephen did not need his wallet for his last trip: it was the trip of a lifetime, paid in full by his Lord and Master.

Every year multitudes of Christians are persecuted for their faith and thousands killed, most proclaiming Christ to the end. Why is it that so many in the West who claim to be Christian go to such great lengths to retain their youth and beauty and to stay alive, no matter the cost? Why are so many afraid of what lies ahead and of their own deaths? If Christians are who they say they are, they should not fear death. There is no fear when Jesus is your Savior, you know God as your Father, and you believe the Bible to be his Word.

ASSURANCE

Without hope we relinquish the joy of living, and hopelessness ensues. Even when a Christian is dying, there is hope—the ultimate hope—of eternal life. Their loved ones, too, have this hope, if they are believers. Christians count everything as joy, even trials, as the testing of our faith brings perseverance. Our heartaches and heartbreaks perfect our faith. God uses every heartache to bring us closer to him. Christ's blood washes away all the sin that we repent of through his atoning sacrifice of love. His saving grace does not remove our memories of past sins or regret, but it covers them so that we may face God spotless, white as snow, as though we had not erred. With the knowledge of our full assurance and pardon, and the indwelling Holy Spirit, we never forget the cost of our forgiveness.

EXPECTATION IN THE LAST DAYS

Faithful Christians know that Jesus will return one day for his bride. Eternity in heaven with Jesus and with all believers is ensured, although what that may entail is mystery to us. The reality of what Christians may have to face before Jesus's second coming may be horrific and terrifying, but we are commanded to hold fast in our faith and trust God.

We are told repeatedly in the Bible that, just as there were famines of hearing God's voice thousands of years ago, in the last days there will be another great falling away from the Word of God and the way of life that God intended. These days will mean a difficult life for Christians, but we are to take heart. Amos 8:11–12 reveals that people will wander from sea to sea and north to east to seek the word of God, but they will not find it. Our only hope is to store God's Word in our hearts. Many modern preachers and writers have predicted what these last days will look like, but we do not know the specifics. We are, however, to be aware of the signs and to prepare for what is to come. The signs of biblical prophecy indicate that we are in the last days in terms of the world as we know it, but we must continue to live each day for God and not in fear of what may come.

On my third trip to Israel, September 22 to October 8, 2015, I was awestruck by a five-meter-long, white wedding dress floating over the Tower of David, or the Jerusalem Citadel, as it is also called. The dress, part of the installation called "Betrothal," hung over the main exhibition area of the Tower of David, just outside the gate to my hotel and across from the Jaffa Gate in the Old City of Jerusalem. It was part of the Second Jerusalem Biennale for Contemporary Jewish Art that began September 24. Those in Jerusalem for Sukkot, for conferences, or to view the fourth in the tetrad of blood moons were both surprised and intrigued by this beautiful dress hanging over the city. The display was prophetic for both Jews and Christians. For the Jews, the dress represented the anticipated arrival of their Messiah, God, the husband coming for the betrothed, his chosen people. It was even more significant for those Christians who witnessed it, because they wait patiently for the second coming of Christ, when he will bring all the faithful who have died and then be united with his church, the bride.

Although I know that God is always with me, I do not expect a good earthly existence because I follow Jesus. My ultimate expectation is of an eternal spiritual existence with Jesus and loved ones. I expect to see him in all of his glory either when I die or when he returns.

**Wedding dress over Jerusalem, Tower of
David, September-October 2015**

CHAPTER 11

D: DEDICATION TO GOD

Whatever you do, work heartily, as for the Lord and not for men, knowing that from the Lord you will receive the inheritance as your reward. You are serving the Lord Christ. (Colossians 3:23–24)

With eternity assured through Jesus and knowing the only God, Creator of this mighty universe through the Bible, I live with him as my fortress and strength in the power of the Holy Spirit. I do not live for myself or to please another person. I live in devotion and obedience to God's will, to please and serve him, worshipping and fellowshipping with him. There is only one way to live for him: his way, in his power and strength. A believer's security comes from living God's ways in his Word, by his power, and in his will.

Although the name of Jesus rolls casually off many tongues, he is far from them. Jesus must be in our hearts, on our minds, and master over our lives. Some try to please God in worldly ways, thinking they are achieving something for him, while living lives outside his will. Some dedicate themselves to teaching and preaching fallible interpretations of his Word. The inerrant Bible unites all who are faithful to God. The Bible *is* God's way.

Unless we have been totally convinced of God's truth, we cannot be sure that we are worshipping the one true God, and we have little hope of ever discerning his will. Only God can do this. The devil wants us to stay grounded in the world—his territory. Contending with the ever-present interference and static of the enemy, God's way means that we use the Bible as our sole source to remain in God's will and to combat the devil.

WISDOM IS GOD'S WILL

After our hearts are circumcised by God, we seek after the things God desires. Because the Holy Spirit indwells us, not even death troubles us. Living to please God alone, with our hearts firmly trusting in him, we are secure. God offers all that we need to live a godly life in expectation of eternity. As our hearts are turned toward God, and we are grieved for the things that grieve him, when a sinful thought, word, or deed comes to mind, our hearts are immediately brought before the throne of Almighty God in repentance. We know what grieves God, and we do not want to grieve him or the Holy Spirit. We know that he is forever with us and his Spirit indwelling us, unless we blaspheme the Holy Spirit. We do not want him to leave us and we will do nothing to cause him to leave: our lives become one constant, formidable prayer.

All of us are susceptible to temptation, error, and sin. In order to even want to follow God's will, we have to know what that actually is, not what people think it is. We do not follow God's will when we hold to strict orthodox manmade teachings in some areas, while casting a blind eye or holding to a liberal interpretation of the Bible in other areas. All sin is hurtful to God, sexual sin especially so, and the only way for us to know what God wants is to know what he says about sin and to carry it inside us. We will only find favor in his sight when we are faithfully doing everything we can to live according to his standards, not ours or the world's.

Knowing what is of God is key to being dedicated to Him, for we cannot be true to God if we do not live as he tells us to live. Christians are called to trust in God alone with all of their hearts and live by his Word alone. By trusting in one passage of the Bible to inform our understanding of other passages, we learn how undeniably true the Word of God is. We acknowledge God in everything we do; we are nothing outside of him. When we see his truth revealed, it is easier to be in awe of him, and turn from evil. The Holy Spirit writes the truth on the tablets of our hearts when we submit to him. We must be sensitive to what pleases God and allow these things to become part of who we are; apart from him, we are wicked. Knowing God's wisdom is his will for believers.

The Bible has impacted the whole world like no other book ever has. It laid foundations for education, literature, hospitals, science, technology, human freedom, and equality. Christians have no secret knowledge, but they know that they can never be wise apart from God. The only true knowledge about God comes from the Bible. If we seek out the words of men, we will have a faulty foundation on which to base our faith and trust in God. God, in his supreme wisdom, provided his Word miraculously through humans.

Before I studied the Bible, I had a good but incomplete life. Many consider themselves wise yet have never read the Bible. It is impossible to know God's will or understand him outside the Bible. Bibles are easy to obtain, but in the West they are rarely read. Many people search for greater meaning to their lives, but they are being sidetracked by the very things the Bible warns us to avoid. How can we know God's will if we have not read his only instruction book? How can we understand what others write about the Bible if we have never studied it? It is outside the will of God to be ignorant of his Word and to our peril if we are.

DISCERNING GOD'S WILL

God has a plan for every life, and he desires that all come to him. As a new Christian is born, the narrow gate to eternal life opens. With soft, pliable hearts, our desire to grow closer to God and our earnest pleas to grow closer to him through prayer and Bible reading takes on a transcendent meaning. Gradually, a selfish, personal will is replaced by God's will. A person will understand the Bible in varying degrees and levels commensurate with the condition of the heart and with the amount of time given to reading, praying about, and studying it. Once we are saved, we begin to love and understand God's Word; as we obey, we are drawn to further prayer, study, and sanctification.

Many things that seemed innocent I now see differently in the light of God's Word. I see how culture encourages dreams and aspirations, built on society's definition of body image, wealth, material possessions, intimacy, sexuality, magic, and fantasy. Today, with social media and "reality" television, the world can literally watch you live your life as it is staged. Some are content to observe others live; others want to be famous. Life at center-stage is like life in a fishbowl, yet many desire to live this way, as evidenced by Facebook and other social media sites. Cellphones can dictate who many believe themselves to be and this can jeopardize the development of healthy self-concepts and self-confidence. The World Wide Web is aptly named; as a web, it lures and traps its prey. The Internet is a valuable tool, and can be a worthwhile aid to understanding God and his Word, but in using it caution is necessary, because it has an eternal memory.

The Bible cautions us to be wise as serpents and innocent as doves. Innocence also involves loving wisely as God does. I enjoy investigative journalism, but I critique what is being reported. Some readers adopt what is in print, on the air, and on social media as truth and do not critically evaluate their thinking, to their spiritual detriment. Western society excessively critiques zoos, nature parks, hunting and fishing, and anything which is perceived as restricting nature, while at the same time openly displaying human beings on reality shows. Twenty-first-century displays may differ in presentation from what Abraham Ulrikab's family experienced one hundred and thirty years ago, but their purpose is no different. Social media has generated a new cultural mindset, dictating how people interact with one another. Some, addicted to online interaction, collect cyber followers that reinforce their worldview and, in doing so, provide them with a new identity and sense of self-worth. Some of these web denizens are, ironically, degraded and disliked by their followers. Life in the twenty-first century proves how important it is to always test and discern what is the will of God, if we say we are his, regardless of what the world may think or say.

Being wise, gentle, loving, and innocent is impossible in our own strength. A small but wise and discerning group of fellow Christians who pray for each other and hold one another accountable is a valuable God-given gift in upholding godly faithful standards. When we believe in God, our awe and fear of him is the beginning of wisdom and turning away from evil shows him our personal growth in knowledge and discernment. So many today stand in awe of mere mortals: sports heroes, entertainers, movie stars, reality- show stars, and television personalities. However, not many are in awe of God. The Bible teaches us we are to fear and be in awe of him. We are to fear him, stand in awe of his mercy and goodness, and serve him faithfully while considering all that he has done for us.

LOVING AND OBEYING GOD

Some think God is arrogant to order us to love him. How can we love on demand? We cannot. But we are talking about the God of all creation, who created us. God can command what he desires to command. We have the choice to love him or not. That means a drastic change of heart, either instantaneously or gradually, requiring obedience to him, service to him, and aligning our wills with his.

When we choose to love God and that love for him and his Word grows stronger each day, we are still open to sin and to falling away from his will. We become convicted about things which in the past seemed appropriate but are no longer acceptable to us as children of God. We begin to see everything through the lens of God's Word. Suddenly we find ourselves wondering what God thinks. The Holy Spirit constantly helps us see things God's way. We consult the Bible and pray for his guidance. Without our fully realizing what is happening, we are being transformed as our hearts are being sanctified, and we want to obey God because we love him.

Many new believers testify as to how easy it was to follow God once they were saved. Some witness how sins and addictions miraculously fell away as they were convicted of the truth of the gospel. However, even when we are steeped in prayer and God's Word and supported by fellow Christians, falling back into old habits can easily happen as believers are tempted to sin.

To Whom Much Is Given

As I recall the broken glass and the January 2008 meeting, I remember that even up until the clergy was congregated and ready to sign the document I encouraged Stephen to sign it. But, seated in church, maybe as a result of pondering my prayers to God at the time of the glass incident, I prayed that he would not sign it. My heart cried out, *We are God's alone.* What we do in the earthly realm does have spiritual consequences. As Stephen went forward, I begged him silently, *No, don't sign it. Jesus Christ is the head of the church. He is the one we answer to. He is the only one whose counsel we should seek.* The apostles believed this. I believe it. Stephen signed the document. The incident impacted me, provoking much thought and prayer over the ensuing months, but I did not share this with Stephen because it would not have solved anything and would have caused undue stress. I knew God would use it as he willed, but I felt that maybe I had lost an opportunity. I will never know. I put it out of my mind until after Stephen's death.

The Bible sets out clear guidelines for most things but we have instituted so much in our churches that may be outside the will of God. God's Word is silent on some issues, and different interpretations of them lead to confusion. However, there is much clarity if the Bible is taken as the ultimate truth and roadmap for life. God does not make mistakes; we do. God expects our obedience. He knows when we are doing our best, when we miss the mark, and why, when, and if we return to him with contrite hearts.

While in Israel on my third visit just before this book was ready for a second edit, I was convicted of my procrastination in completing this work for God. Luke 12:48 made me realize fully the significance of God's gift of the glass and his communicating to me this way. I know that I will be held accountable for all that God has entrusted me. I wondered if I was being unfaithful or if God was holding me back for his timing to be right.

To serve God, be dedicated to his will, and work with the same willing, loving heart as Jesus did entails using the Bible, the very words of God, as our guide, as Jesus did and taught, while serving through the strength of the Holy Spirit. We are told to serve God with gladness, to serve with our whole hearts, as if we were serving Jesus, not people. This is how we serve the least of these, Jesus said, when we feed the hungry and visit the sick and those in prison, we do it to him. But we can only serve fully if we trust him fully. I knew I was beginning to trust Jesus fully with everyone and everything in my life.

I am thankful for all that God has done for me. Through my trust in God and his Word, service flows out of passionate love for him through Christ. All around me lies opportunity to serve and witness. I see these possibilities with new eyes, as I have a much greater compassion for the eternal well-being of the souls of others. My prayer is for strength and resources to continually reach out and serve as God directs, leads, and guides.

RELINQUISHING MY WILL FOR HIS

We totally trust God by leaning on him. Fully trusting God and relinquishing my will for his has been the most difficult aspect of faith for me. As I watched Stephen's trust in God grow, especially during our retreat in Mexico in February-March 2010, I could see that his heart was far ahead of mine in this aspect. We had deep discussions around trusting and accepting God's will during that time of spiritual growth and refreshment. Stephen normally did not do a lot of personal writing at home but when he did he always had much to say. This excerpt from his journal for Saturday, February 27, 2010, speaks of his growing faith in God:

> In living each day with actions and decisions and thoughts directed at exalting Christ as Lord both in our hearts as the motivation and response for living and as a witness to all others that they may see, hear, experience, and know the awesome trust and reality that can only be found in Christ, the Risen Lord and Savior Redeemer of the world. We see, we understand that the outward social and cultural worldly values of life's journey are of no lasting substance, they are temporal and fleeting. So we trust in God's work and vision to draw all things into Christ and eternity with Christ. There is fullness of life within this life's day-to-day journey and the promise and hope of God's fullest revelation and reality for all believers in the eternal and everlasting world to come with union in Christ, Father and the Holy Spirit.

Stephen knew that what mattered was his faith and trust in Jesus to carry him through our trials. He had accepted God's will and trusted him to know what was best for both of us relative to God's good purposes, including the end of his earthly life. I had a long way to go.

Surrendering Our Wills

The Bible warns us not to use our newly found freedom in Christ as opportunity to enjoy worldly pleasures. If we walk by the Holy Spirit, we will not capitulate to the desires of the flesh; those desires are against the Spirit, and the desires of the Spirit against the flesh. If we live by the Spirit, we will walk in God's will, not our own. This remarkable freedom we have through Christ is to be taken seriously yet with extreme caution. Living in the world and not being of it is difficult, especially if we are not firmly grounded in God's Word and supported by other Bible-believing Christians, because we are constantly tempted to compromise our beliefs and values.

The only true evidence of the presence of the Holy Spirit in a new believer's life is when they cease from an activity they once thought harmless, and enjoyed. God works through recovery programs, but salvation through Christ may result in instantaneous cessation of swearing, smoking, alcohol use, pornography. For Christians, all victory comes from God through the Holy Spirit, but often harmful and sinful behaviors take years to defeat, and some are never completely overcome. A true follower of Christ will never say that something God condemns as sinful is good. *Never.* Believers live for Christ, witness for him, and are appropriate models to nonbelievers by their lives. They read and ingest the Bible thoroughly and honestly and accurately teach it. For God's children commitment to Christ cannot be part-time. All Christians must boldly proclaim and live out the commands in God's Word, realizing that we do not have all the answers or the strength in ourselves to follow God's will.

The do-as-I-say-and-not-as-I-do adage is no longer acceptable in the secular world. It holds no weight in Christianity either, as preachers must be living models, through God's Word that they thoroughly digest and passionately teach. The world watches us and how we deal with all issues. The media is quick to respond, especially when leaders are shown to violate not only biblical but also civil laws. God has helped us overcome sin, and we should be proud to identify him as the reason for the change in us.

God's call on our lives as we align our wills with his is to be beacons of light in a lost and broken world. Where it is darkest in the world his light shines all the brighter through us. God wants us to not only know his will and want to live it but also to actually live and preach his truth as his ambassadors to the world.

A Woman Serving God

Being a woman called to serve God through ordained ministry in the Anglican church created conflict within me because of the conflict in the church over that issue. This caused much soul searching, Bible reading, and pouring out my heart to God. At one point I considered writing about women in vestments, or clerical garments, punning on *investment*. Our society invests in many things, but few invest in things that have eternal meaning. Investing in women as clergy or pastors is rare in Bible-believing communities. Women do wear vestments sometimes as part of the Anglican tradition. Jesus is invested in me just as much as he was in his female disciples and as he is in any male or female today. In fact, he is more invested in people than he is in church buildings or manmade doctrines and traditions.

At the beginning of my theological study, I was so busy being hospitable in my own home that I did not realize that the most important thing I could do was to read and study the very book our faith was built upon—the Bible. I am now better equipped to be used by God, including teaching all who desire to know more of God's Word, even my children and grandchildren. Through sitting at Jesus's feet came many questions, but even more answers. I had retired from a teaching career but I felt God's call upon my life so strongly that I was unable to do anything else. After Stephen's death I began to study the Old Testament, and through God's command to do so I am determined to understand more of it.

In 2010 after my thesis was published and I was ordained to the diaconate, Stephen told me he thought he had fulfilled his mission in life: to get me started in the ministry. I was shocked and rather upset by his revelation; I wanted both of us to be in ministry together, and I knew he was telling me he felt that he would not be alive much longer. I felt honored but at the same time heartbroken, with a heavy weight of responsibility. How I live my life for Jesus in a world of hypocrisy and sin is paramount. As a church leader it is necessary that I live within God's will for my life but also because the sin of those in ministry will be judged more severely. My desire is to serve God with my whole heart and with a willing mind.

Both man and woman, made in God's image, were created good. Yet both sinned and fell short of the glory of God. Even though the Bible tells us not to worry about what we eat or what we wear, for so many Christians, diet, body image, exercise, and fashion seem to dominate much of our time, far more than studying the Bible or loving God. They did for me for far too long. As the temple of God, and of the Holy Spirit, we are to care for these earthen jars we inhabit, but we are not to show excessive concern over clothing, food, and physique, while at the same time showing so little discernment about what we read, watch, listen to, do, or say. We must discern God's will about our choices regarding our own bodies and what we do. We are to glorify God in everything. We know that, as believers, we should live God's way, but the world lures us into thinking that looking good and overtly displaying our sexuality is necessary to be an accepted twenty-first-century person; this creates tension in us. Current women's issues matter a great deal to me as a Christian woman and should concern all Christians, male and female, as we discern God's will through his Word.

Sometimes relationships become impaired, fractured, and even totally broken during our Christian walk. Not all of these can be sustained, especially if they are spiritually unhealthy, and it may not be God's desire for us to remain in them. Refusing to compromise our primary relationship with God in order to hold worldly relationships with others is a good test of what is most important and one area where learning to listen, heed, and obey the Holy Spirit is wise. I was blessed by two wonderful marriages. Both times my heart ached when my husband died, and God comforted and supported me. I will see Corb and Stephen again, not as my husbands but as God's children, as part of the family of God, with perfected bodies.

Sexuality and sensuality dominate many Christians' lives. Sex is a gift from God and to be enjoyed within God's parameters. It is, however, a god for some Christians, some of whom have fallen prey to lust and pornography, for instance, becoming more famous for their error than for their faith. Not one of us is free from temptation, and unless we dress in the complete armor of God daily, we may find ourselves dealing with far more than we can handle on our own. When we leave God outside the door of anything, he still sees and hears, and he may choose to leave us to our own devices.

I only came to the full realization of who I am, while struggling to exist and serve God, by knowing, loving, and honoring God before all others. As a child of God, but also a mother and grandmother, I know giving birth to be a wonderful privilege and raising children a tremendous responsibility; however, being a Christian role model to all I come in contact with is even more so. God wants us to treat people with respect, dignity, and love. That does not mean we are always full of false flattery. God wants us to speak his truth with his love. Using either half of the equation alone is equally displeasing to him. God's truth without his love may not bear as much fruit, while his love without his truth means little. The distinction between the righteous and the wicked, between those who serve God and those who serve themselves and the world, will eventually be brought to his light. Christian women can lessen the suffering and plight of the masses of the third world, the poor, the ravaged, and the starving. God's call on my life is to reach the lost with his Word in all parts of the world. But often before we can distribute Bibles to some, we first have to meet their physical needs.

DEDICATED TO GOD'S WAYS

Life is not all about us. It is all about God and his will for eternity. We must constantly guard against the sins of self-righteousness, pride, and selfishness. In church leadership, role models and standards are important, yet too often good Christian examples are lacking.

Throughout theological studies, and then later through personal biblical study, I learned how much Jesus loved women, not only his mother but Martha and her sister, Mary, the woman at the well, the woman caught in adultery, and those women who supported his ministry, his benefactors, and the women who first saw him at the tomb. Many women have been and continue to be pillars of their faith communities. Many of the Labrador Moravian missionaries were female. Rachel Saint, sister of Nate Saint, one of five MAF martyrs, returned with other women to Ecuador in 1955 after the tragedy, and many Waodani were saved. Corrie ten Boom (1982–1983), a Dutch Christian, mobilized her family to help many Jews escape the Nazis in World War II. There were, and are, many such women. There is a valuable place for women in ministry. There is much work to be done by ethical, Christ-like, and modest women who will serve God with compassion and humility. The church—men and women—must teach God's Word in love.

Following Christ gives us hope because we are all broken, apart from God and his Son. There is joy in living a life worthy of the God who made us. In order for us to fulfil God's plan for our lives and help spread the gospel, we must be committed to him, his Word, and Christ, who makes us whole. Through my dedication to God, I have the freedom to minister wholeheartedly to others as he directs. Everything I do must be done as if done for him—not because it looks good or pleases people. The hearts of true Christians are dedicated to God and discerning his will. With the great commandment and the great commission as guides, the Holy Spirit prepares the way for the dedicated service of those whose hearts have been circumcised and are ready, willing, and able to serve God.

The heart and the glass

CHAPTER 12

❧: THE CIRCUMCISED HEART: READY, IMPERFECT, SOFTENED, TRANSPARENT

> So we do not lose heart. Though our outer self is wasting away, our inner self is being renewed day by day. For this light momentary affliction is preparing for us an eternal weight of glory beyond all comparison, as we look not to the things that are seen but to the things that are unseen. For the things that are seen are transient, but the things that are unseen are eternal. (2 Corinthians 4:16–18)

"*Y*et even now," declares God, "return to me with all your heart, with fasting, with weeping, and with mourning; and rend your hearts and not your garments" (Joel 2:12–13a). A circumcised heart is turned toward God, loving him completely. The prophet Joel called sinful Judah to grieve like betrothed virgins whose promised husbands had died before their marriages were consummated might grieve. Instead of tearing sackcloth in their lament, they were to repent of their sin and turn back to God. To love him, follow his ways, and repent of their sin was God's desire for the Israelites of Joel's day. Such passages reminded the wayward Jewish nation of their sin so that they might learn from it, return to God, and obey him, but they also apply to those of us desiring a relationship with him through Jesus today.

God implores us all to accept Jesus as Lord and Savior, to be his child and to trust, love, and obey him. God is gracious, kind, and desires that we choose him as he chose us. It is never too late, while we draw breath, to say yes. God's Word emphasizes the importance of the condition of our hearts, which house far more than emotions, character, and personality. They are the totality of our being. God is forever declaring the desires of his heart so that all might come to him. He wants to work on, and in, our hearts so that we may turn to him and live forever in the wholeness of his grace.

Jesus was right there in front of Israel all of the time, and yet, when he came to them, they did not know who he was. For many of us today, he is there in the pages of the Bible, yet we do not want to be his. Still God is perfectly patient, always looking for the stray sheep to draw into the fold, ready to forgive his imperfect children when they are ready to accept his Son. There is no love in the universe comparable to the love of God. When we open our hearts to his transformational power, submit to his ways, and permit him to sanctify us, we are changed, and forever his. He rejoices in everyone who covenants with him. God's heart is broken for the world today just as it was in the days of Joel.

If we are God's, there will be much fruit, much evidence of the circumcision of our hearts. We will have been justified, regenerated, transformed, in the process of sanctification, filled with overflowing godly love, and we will be made more holy and righteous with every passing day. God does not want our sacrifices, meaningless traditions, or empty words. He does not want our rituals or impersonal rhetoric. He does not want our legalistic or holier-than-thou attitudes. God wants our hearts.

A Drastic Change of Heart

Over six hundred years before the birth of Christ the prophet Jeremiah knew that the condition of the people's hearts was not right. Although the Israelites were often obedient to God, circumcising their flesh, their hearts were far from him. Jeremiah had a difficult life, as did most of the faithful prophets. Jeremiah's calling people to repentance while he taught at the temple elicited much persecution. He warned repeatedly of the consequences of uncircumcised hearts. Jeremiah's courage was admired by the apostle Paul, who preached on the need to write on tablets of human hearts in 2 Corinthians 3:2–3. Both Jeremiah and Paul strove to bring people back to loving and obeying God. Unlike Paul, according to the Bible and other historical sources, Jeremiah's preaching apparently only ever convicted Baruck, his faithful secretary, and led to his repentance, and an Ethiopian eunuch who served King Zedekiah, but his words have impacted and changed many over the centuries. Jeremiah stood firm in God's truth.

It is through the faith and persistence of people like Jeremiah that we have written records of the tumultuous times in which they lived. These records show that the personal disobedience of the people often resulted in their experiencing their own demise, their own "great and terrible day of the Lord," as Joel 2:31 describes it. The hardness of their hearts and their turning away from God meant their own annihilation. The Bible is a gift from God, who used such men as Jeremiah and Paul. Through the power of the Holy Spirit they reveal to us what God desires: turning away from our sinful ways and turning to him.

Although we live in a far different world from that of Moses, Jeremiah, Paul, and the saints of the early church, in many ways we are united by the condition of our hearts. Our hearts are either hardened, turned away from God, or soft, pliable, but still imperfect, and turned to God, eager to have the Holy Spirit transform them. We learn from Jeremiah and Paul the importance of the heart condition. Tough, hardened hearts do not provide fertile soil for God's Word to germinate in, nor for the Holy Spirit to nourish. Human hearts require and receive softening to the time of death; glorification cannot be achieved on earth.

Circumcision of the heart, like the Old Testament covenant of circumcision, is more difficult for some than for others. Although circumcision occurs at the moment of salvation, the skillful maneuvering of the Holy Spirit's sword is constantly at work sanctifying us. In a willing and obedient heart, the sanctification process still may be extremely painful as deep roots of accumulated, hardened flesh and embedded sin must be cut away.

Jesus knew God, his Father, directly, yet he thoroughly knew the Old Testament and always taught from it. He knew it better than the scribes and Pharisees of his day. If Jesus, the Son of God, used God's Word for teaching, edification, and rebuke, we must also use it and value it, above all else, as he did. A circumcised heart realizes, truly appreciates, and grows to love the enormous wealth found in God's Word. We must give the Bible the place of honor it deserves, never adding to or taking away from it. God blesses our reading, study, and meditation on his Word. Streams of living water flow refreshingly from it, reviving and cleansing us. I have seen the wonderful changes wrought in the hearts of those who have read and studied God's Word. The more and harder they study, the greater the changes are, and the softer their hearts and greater their love for others.

READINESS IS ESSENTIAL

Today is no different from biblical days. Many believed then, as now, that their future was in their own hands or with their pagan gods, who could be appeased. Today, if a person is talented, and/or skilled, in terms of sports, music, and art, or has financial or political prowess, he or she can fulfil big dreams. Some believe they make their own quality of life and so live lives of self-sufficiency. Others thank God, believing they have been blessed because they have pleased God or because of hard work; still others act as if they themselves have become God. All humans have the choice to love God as he commands, to believe or ignore him, or to say that he does not exist. We all will be held accountable for our choice one day.

God cautions us that if anyone loves the world his love is not in him or her. Although we are each born into a unique set of circumstances, in the free, democratic world the prevalent mindset is that the underdog can become the top dog, the underachiever can become the overcomer with hard work—referred to as the American dream. In recent years gambling and high-risk, high-profit, lucrative businesses, both legal and illegal, bring wealth; the sky is the limit, work ethic may not be as important as luck, and God is left totally out of the picture. Yet when we find we are in over our heads, it is easy to blame it all on God. In order for us to be God's children we must be ready, want to change, ask for it, and accept his will for our lives as our own.

We must believe on the Lord Jesus Christ as our Savior and accept God's offer to be his child and to the gift of eternal life. After that, the Holy Spirit indwells us, and God uses the Holy Spirit first to circumcise our hearts and then to transform us into a different being, a whole new creation. God's arms are always open for us to turn from our sinful ways. God joyfully welcomes anyone who takes that first step to him, accepts his Son, Jesus, and calls him Father.

IMPERFECT—SANCTIFICATION PROCEEDING

Everyone who believes that Jesus is the Christ has been born of God and everyone who loves the Father loves whoever has been born of him. We know we are the children of God when we love him and obey his commandments. We must live in this world and not be of it. Although we may seek the holiness and righteousness of God, we know that it cannot be fully found in this life. We grow closer to him as we faithfully pray and read the Bible. God has his ways of growing us, keeping us humble, and allowing us to slip and fall from time to time. One of the greatest changes in my own heart, as I have sought to draw closer to God, is that it is much easier to be true to him and much more difficult to deny him, or pretend he does not exist.

A mature Christian is still a target for sin. No matter how godly a Christian becomes, we remain a sinner until death, one who will at times give in to temptation and will need to repent of sin to be forgiven. As believers, we know where to find wise Christian counsel though, both through God's Word and through other believers. Our trust is always in God through Jesus; in ourselves we can never obey his laws and commandments. We do, however, conscientiously and consistently seek God, as Jesus did. We will pursue holiness and righteousness but know they cannot be attained. To think we are better than anyone else is prideful; to think we have it all right is to wallow in self-righteousness. We delight in God's laws and ways as we meditate on the Bible day and night, and until we die, we are being sanctified to be more like Christ.

Softening—The Holy Spirit at Work

Jesus is the vine, we are branches. We can do nothing apart from him. All that makes the heart sick—the sludge, the dross, the decay, the sharp and rough edges—is cut away when we are saved. God knows when the heart is penitent and wants to be circumcised. He knows when a person wants to please him. He knows, has mercy, and saves through his perfect grace. The justified heart is softer, but continual softening is part of the sanctification process until we die.

God knows those who trust him, because they have a heart for what he has a heart for—they empathize with the poor, the sick, the lost, and the imprisoned. Those whose hearts are being softened are eager to share the gospel of Jesus Christ. They serve God, and disciple others into serving him too. But mostly they will be known by their genuine love for humanity—a love that is totally honest, not cutting; totally caring, not judgmental; totally concerned, not prying. They will know, as James taught, that faith by itself, if it does not have works, is dead. Faith with good work is trust. I have prayed for trust in God as Jesus trusted him, and it has come.

I seek after Christ and God's Word, because only God makes me whole. My attitude toward my Creator must be right; otherwise I am out of his will for my life. He did not come to make me happy or give me a good life. He came to rescue me from my fallen, sinful self and to make me whole in him. As my heart is softened, I have a new understanding of life and its purpose.

We know that in this world we will have trials and tribulations. As fallen rebellious creatures, we will never achieve holiness, no matter how hard we try. Christians know whom to follow. Jesus alone saves souls. But by his Spirit we can do all things through him who strengthens us, if we follow his example and are obedient to the Father.

God comforts the heavy-hearted, the persecuted, and the grieving, and he blesses those who seek his will. The blessings he brings are many, but we follow him because we love him, not to receive blessings. Although God does mightily bless us sometimes, at other times we are being tempted beyond our ability to resist, and attacked more than we can bear. Other times our burdens and trials may just be too much for us on our own, but God, through the Holy Spirit, Christian friends, and even angels, comes to our spiritual rescue to bear us up, so that we may be softened even further.

A TRANSPARENT HEART

One of the most important marks of a heart willing and wanting to be sanctified into the image of Christ's heart is that of total transparency and honesty. God detests lies and dishonesty. Honesty is foundational to the circumcised heart's being sanctified. Jesus was totally honest, even to the point of death. He could not lie to save his life; neither should we. God can work in us when we are not honest, but we only begin to see results when we are completely honest with others and ourselves. Honesty is essential to a softened heart and flows from it. Today the definition of honesty has been so stretched that it stands for almost nothing. When being totally forthright becomes unwise or dangerous for Christians, God will intervene and ensure safety if it is his will to do so. We must trust him unreservedly, as we know we are always safe when we are his.

Total transparency sometimes creates tension in a world that does not promote honesty, but it is impossible to compromise on God's Word. Only it lasts forever; only it is to be trusted to lead and direct us. When we are truly God's, given over to his will, we have far greater peace with him, with ourselves, with our families, and with the world, because we know that God is in control and we need worry about nothing. We know that everything will come in his perfect timing and way. All we need to do is to be faithful, loving God, being obedient, and lifting up our hearts to him in regular prayer. We need to trust God. The prophet Micah has told us what is good: God requires that we be just and kind and to walk humbly with him (Micah 6:8).

God's Truth Sets Us Free

God guides and blesses us in our personal Bible study by the power of the Holy Spirit, increasing our knowledge and understanding of his ways to aid us in leading people to him. When we immerse ourselves in both the Old and New Testaments, the Holy Spirit helps us to be obedient to God. We must pray for God's direction and guidance in teaching his truth accurately and for protection against heresy, laziness, pride, self-righteousness, and legalism. Bible study is precious holy work. Each teacher of the Bible is held accountable to the same high standard God holds all church leaders.

I finally acquiesced to God's command to read and study the Old Testament and I have been blessed phenomenally. I have learned that all accounts in it, from creation to Noah, Abraham and God's covenant with Israel (four thousand years ago approximately), Moses, the Law and Passover (three thousand and five hundred years ago approximately), David, his sin and his heart for God (three thousand years ago approximately), Daniel and his courage (two thousand and six hundred years ago approximately), through countless faithful prophets, judges, kings, men, and women all point to Jesus in the New Covenant. The Bible is to be honored, studied, and taught respectfully for what it is—the very Word of God. The truth of God's Word sets us free as nothing else can because we know the source of eternal wealth that surpasses and defies any worldly definition.

Through my poring over the Bible I developed seven points as overriding precepts to guide my study and teaching.

1. **God is the great I Am. He always was, is, and forever will be, holy.** God is mighty, worthy of our worship, reverential fear, and awe. He is the only uncreated, perfect Being, and there is no one like God. I am not in God's category. "The fear of the Lord is the beginning of wisdom, and the knowledge of the Holy One is insight" (Proverbs 9:10).

2. **God reveals himself in his Word, the Bible.** The Old Testament was the Bible Jesus knew and taught from. Together the Old and New Testaments comprise God's story of himself, revealing who he is, his purposes, and his desires for his children. It is the only document God inspired and gave us to help us grow to know and love him better. "Your Word is a lamp to my feet and a light to my path" (Psalms 119:105).

3. **God is perfect in three equal, yet distinct divine persons: Father, Son, and Holy Spirit.** Through hearing, reading, and meditating on the Bible, we begin to understand the Godhead in his Divine Trinity as God the Father; God the Son, Savior, and Master; and God the Holy Spirit, Comforter, and Guide. "Go therefore and make disciples of all nations, baptizing them in the name of the Father and of the Son and of the Holy Spirit" (Matthew 28:19).

4. **God, righteous, holy, and sinless, abhors sin.** After the fall, humans disobeyed and were separated from God because of their sin. Through his Word, God warned them to turn back, but they were unable to do it in their own

strength. Only God saves. "For as in Adam all die, so also in Christ shall all be made alive" (1 Corinthians 15:22).

5. **God is made known to us through Jesus, the Word made flesh.** God, who lovingly made humans in his image, desired them to love him as his children. He chose his Son, Jesus, the spotless Lamb, to atone for all who call upon Jesus in repentance and truth. "For God so loved the world, that he gave his only Son, that whoever believes in him should not perish but have eternal life" (John 3:16).

6. **God the Son, Jesus, is as fully human as he is fully divine.** Jesus is the only suitable substitution for us; although he was fully man, he did not sin, but withstood all temptation through praying to God the Father and studying, knowing, and teaching his Word. "For in him the whole fullness of deity dwells bodily" (Colossians 2:9).

7. **God the Holy Spirit will help us become the children of God he created us to be.** When we accept Jesus as Lord and Savior, the power of the Holy Spirit indwells us and helps us become the person God created us to be. Believers are new persons through Christ, not in anything they do themselves. "And those who belong to Christ Jesus have crucified the flesh with its passions and desires" (Galatians 5:24).

GOD'S TRUTH BRINGS JOY, PEACE, LOVE, AND HOPE

My joy has never been reliant on substances that dull the senses or ease unpleasant feelings, but it was and is tied to relationships with, and acceptance by, other people. I idolized some family members, especially Grandmother Vokey, Corb, and my children. Through the Bible I learned that only God is to be worshipped and fully trusted. Only God brings joy. Surrendering to God has brought a joy-filled life despite challenges. Trusting God leads me to make better choices, although temptation and sin are never far away. If I do not repent, sin clouds my ability to feel God's presence; therefore, I repent soon after the Holy Spirit convicts me of sin. Acknowledging sin against God and others, repenting, and being forgiven allow true joy to issue from a loving heart that is not bitter or judgmental, nor does it harbor resentment, or seek revenge.

Some people feel less certain of God and their eternal security as they age, but I thank God that my life has made far more sense in recent years, as I now see everything working together like a giant tapestry. As a young child I remember my grandmother telling me about the great world wars and about men who lied about their age to fight in World War I. Tragically, without training, they were sent to fight, and some were killed their first day on the battlefield. I remember one of my grandmother's strange sayings, "There was only the Turks, n'er a Christian around." As a child I did not have a clue what this meant. The one thing I had heard that sounded anything like Turks had to do with Turkish Delight chocolate bars. When I travelled with a group from Australia and New Zealand on my third trip to Israel, in 2015, my curiosity was piqued about the Royal Newfoundland Regiment, especially with regard to the ANZAC (Australian and New Zealand Army Corps) and the Australian Light Brigade, who had fought with the Royal Newfoundland Regiment in Gallipoli in 1916. Upon returning to St. John's and hearing a presentation about World War I events in Turkey, I learned that the Newfoundland and Turkish soldiers referred to each other as Christians and Turks. My grandmother's words from all those years back now made sense to me. Joy comes for me in understanding why—connections made and error corrected.

God knows those who have passion for what he has passion for.

He knows the patient, the persistent, the longsuffering, and those with the gift of perseverance. He knows those who trust him, because they have a heart for what he has a heart for—they empathize with the poor, the sick, and the lost. Joy comes in knowing that God is in control and leading you to be who he desires you to be as he sanctifies you.

How can I know and be sure that I have a passion for what God has passion for? I know because I believe that the Bible is God's inspired, authoritative Word, which is profitable for teaching, training, and knowing who God is. I have joy in knowing that I am working with God, not against him.

EACH CHILD OF GOD HAS A CIRCUMCISED HEART

It is impossible to fully understand the New Testament without understanding the Old Testament. Because of Jesus's sacrifice on the cross, we can draw near to God without the ritual of animal sacrifice, as was instituted in the Old Testament. Our salvation is assured. It does not rest on anything but belief in the crucified Christ. We are called to love God with our whole hearts: we must turn from sin and strive for perfection, knowing that sinlessness is not possible for us. With changed hearts we form the Body of Christ and support one another in the goal of holiness. The Body of Christ is to hold each individual, especially leaders, accountable to God by teaching the fullness of his Word. In this way each of us is held accountable by the other, while the corporate body stands for God's truth grounded in the Bible.

Our free will permits us to eat, drink, and do what is unhealthy, play what and where it is unsafe, and partake in all sorts of risky behaviors. A world where God healed every illness, prevented every accident, and stopped every mistake before it happened is a fairytale world. However, a life without God has no happy ending. We are in chaos and confusion because we are rebellious. Few desire the loss of our independence, but independence from God is tragic. I rely on God to be who he says he is in the Bible.

We may never understand this side of heaven why God heals some and not others, but he has a reason for everything. He has given us free will, but he weaves all circumstances together for the good of those who love and follow him. As Christians, we need not fear the inexplicable; Jesus told us he would never leave us nor forsake us. There is much beyond our understanding.

There really are only two important questions: Where did I come from? What is my purpose? I know I did not create myself. My intellect does not allow me to believe I just happened or evolved from a primordial soup. After contemplating this for much of my life, and having wavered back and forth, I realized about twenty-five to thirty years ago that I do have a creator who loves me with a perfect love. God desires that I love him with all of my heart, soul, and spirit. I have relinquished it all to him. Through the power of the Holy Spirit, I have established fully, and firmly implanted within the essence of my being, *Yes, there is a creator God, whose heart has broken for me every time that my heart was broken.* As much as I may like to, I cannot reconcile Jesus Christ with all other gods. If Jesus is God, he cannot be reconciled with other faiths, as he himself said that he is the only way.

My lifetime of questioning and seeking after this Being who loves me, and will not let me go, this Son of God sent to earth to redeem us because we could not redeem ourselves—he is the one and only true God. I give all thanks, honor, and glory to Jesus Christ, my Lord and Savior, and to the Bible, God's Living Word, and constant companion of all seeking to know God through the power of the Holy Spirit. The Bible, perfectly complete in itself, is his story.

THE CIRCUMCISED HEART

God desires that we live fully in Christ in the present, having learned well all that the Bible taught us, while looking forward to the future. Although I understand most of the natural consequences of my life choices and experiences, many unanswered questions remain. When I contemplate the meaning of my existence, I realize that I trusted far less in the world than many do. I sought God with my whole heart and I rejoice in him, declaring his glory, his love, and his marvelous ways. Through who I am and everything I have read, seen, and experienced, I know with certainty that I have a maker who created me and loves me like no person can. He gives me purpose to live fully while I am anticipating a full and glorious eternal life.

No one escapes life without having been manipulated, battered and torn, to some degree. We are often devalued and stigmatized, by age, gender, color, education, economic level, and our physical attributes, sometimes the very things that strengthen us. God, however, values everyone equally. He has chosen all of us. We choose or reject him. Only he can heal every bruise and tear. When we understand his love, we know that he is a constant companion, fully relational with us through the Holy Spirit, and he communicates with us through his Word.

I accepted Jesus Christ in my childhood, at which time my heart was circumcised and opened. Not until I had experienced many adversities was I obedient to God's command to seek him through his Word, especially the Old Testament. I found Jesus there in the ancient texts that I had denied and for which so many had died. I was impetuous and ignored God's ways too long, but he waited patiently, knowing when, how, and why my heart would turn back to him. Through my obedience, the Holy Spirit ironed out some of the rough edges and overgrowth before my hardened heart grew calloused and God hardened it inexorably forever. My heart is circumcised and my will welcomes the Holy Spirit's sanctification of me until I die and meet Jesus face to face.

The circumcised heart is like a perfectly prepared space in the soil for a new plant to take root and grow. It provides exactly the proper conditions for the heart to grow, as David's did, toward God. My heart yearns to be like God's heart, but I know that only in tandem with the Holy Spirit, and relinquishing my will for the will of God, is it ever possible to even come close. Circumcised hearts are led by the Holy Spirit to check their own *character* against God's character. They know, as his children, that their morality should resemble that of their loving Father. They delight in being his children and know that their *identity* is secure in his family.

Putting God first means that all *relationships* are in right and proper order, as he ordained. With a faith that is grown and cultivated into an all-sufficient *childlike trust*, we grow each day more faithful to God, putting our faith into action and trusting him totally as Father, becoming more like the people he created us to be.

Our *unseen priority* is God. Growing closer to him is far more important than what can be seen. The physical world no longer dominates, as *matter* is secondary to the unseen spiritual issues that have eternal significance. Living life means loving others but not to the detriment of loving and obeying God.

We take *courage* in the conviction and clarity that comes only through knowing, following, and modeling Christ as Savior and Lord of our lives. All worldly love and intimacy is based on the *intimacy* that he intentionally holds for us. We love and forgive others as Christ loves and forgives us.

We know that our hearts will continue to be purified throughout our earthly lives, as *sanctification* is a lifelong process. The Christian hope includes a life lived well for Christ in the world with the joyful assurance and full *expectation* of eternal life with him and fellow believers, in his eternal kingdom.

We are *dedicated* to God's will and to the discernment of knowing it through knowing his Word, the Bible. We are prepared and *ready*, fully aware that we are *imperfect*, through hearts that have been *softened*, and by being totally *transparent* in our words and actions in the power of the Holy Spirit, we are being transformed until we die. Our lives are forever changed and being transformed into the people that God created us to be, while we live in the world and serve in it for Christ Jesus.

> For now we see in a mirror dimly, but then face to face.
> Now I know in part; then I shall know fully, even as I
> have been fully known. (1 Corinthians 13:12)

Printed in the United States
By Bookmasters